walking with purpose

Dear Friend,

In a world where women are measured by their beauty, achievements, and possessions, wouldn't it be nice to find a place where you could just be valued for who you are?

That place is here. And you aren't alone. You are about to begin a journey closer to the heart of God. The beautiful thing about Him is that His love doesn't depend on anything you do. You can come, baggage and all, and God is just glad that you came. His mercy is always greater than your failings. His forgiveness and grace are without limit.

God is inviting you to draw near to Him— to drop your burdens at His feet. He's encouraging you to open your heart so He can strengthen and refresh it. This is how the writer of Psalm 119 described God: "You are my hiding place and my shield; I hope in your word." And that's my prayer for you—that you will come to know beyond a doubt that He is your safe place. The more you read His words, the clearer that truth will become.

As you open the pages of Scripture during this study, remember that you are reading God's love letters to you. He waits for you. He doesn't wait because He wants to demand your time. He simply enjoys the presence of His precious daughter—YOU!

With faith in the One who never fails,

Lisa Brenninkmeyer
Founder and Chief Purpose Officer, Walking with Purpose

Living in the Father's Love

A Study of God the Father

www.walkingwithpurpose.com

Authored by Lisa Brenninkmeyer

IMPRIMATUR   +William E. Lori, S.T.D., Archbishop of Baltimore

The recommended Bible translations for use in Walking with Purpose studies are: The New American Bible, which is the translation used in the United States for the readings at Mass; The Revised Standard Version, Catholic Edition; and The Jerusalem Bible.

Any internet addresses (websites, blogs, etc.) in this book are offered as a resource and may change in the future. Please refer to www.walkingwithpurpose.com as the central location for corresponding materials and references.

22 23 24 25 26 / 15 14 13 12

ISBN: 978-1-943173-03-7

Living in the Father's Love: A Study of God the Father
(RSV)

Printed in the United States of America

TABLE OF CONTENTS

INTRODUCTION

LESSONS

APPENDICES

ANSWER KEY

PRAYER PAGES

Welcome to Walking with Purpose

You have many choices when it comes to how you spend your time—thank you for choosing Walking with Purpose. Studying God's Word with an open and receptive heart will bring spiritual growth and enrichment to all aspects of your life, making every moment that you've invested well worth it.

Each one of us comes to this material from our own unique vantage point. You are welcome as you are. No previous experience is necessary. Some of you will find that the questions in this study cause you to think about concepts that are new to you. Others might find much is a review. God meets each one of us where we are, and He is always faithful, taking us to a deeper, better place spiritually, regardless of where we begin.

The Structure of Living in the Father's Love

Living in the Father's Love is a six-session Bible study that integrates Scripture with the teachings of the Roman Catholic Church to help answer the core question, "What kind of a father is God?"

For those who are participating in Walking with Purpose in a group context, four weeks of this study will be spent in small groups discussing one of the lessons from the *Living in the Father's Love Study Guide*. Twice during the study, participants will gather for a Connect Coffee, which consists of social time, a DVD presentation of one of the related Bible study talks, and small group discussion. Those of us who are doing this study on our own will find it simplest to watch the videos online, using the URLs provided with the talk outlines.

Lesson 1: Connect Coffee Talk - The Beauty of a Childlike Faith
Lesson 2: What Kind of a Father Is God?
Lesson 3: What Is the Purpose of My Life?
Lesson 4: How Does God Define Beauty?
Lesson 5: How Do I Work at Forgiving Myself and Others?
Lesson 6: Connect Coffee Talk - Loving Like Him through Forgiveness

Study Guide Format and Reference Materials

The *Living in the Father's Love Study Guide* is divided into three sections:

The first section comprises six lessons. Most lessons are divided into five "days" to help you form a habit of reading and reflecting on God's Word regularly. If you are a woman who has only bits and pieces of time throughout your day to accomplish tasks, you will find this breakdown of the lessons especially helpful. Days One through Four focus on Scripture readings and excerpts from the *Catechism of the Catholic Church*. Day Five includes a story about a saint; a conclusion; a resolution section, in which you set a goal for yourself based on a theme of the lesson; and the portions of the *Catechism of the Catholic Church* that are referenced in the lesson. Each lesson ends with a relevant verse study. Instructions on how to do a verse study can be found in Appendix 2.

For the two Connect Coffee talks in the series, accompanying outlines are offered as guides for taking notes. Included are questions to guide your group's discussion following the talks.

The second section, the appendices, contains supplemental materials referred to during the study, and includes an article about Saint Thérèse of Lisieux, the patron saint of Walking with Purpose.

The third section contains the answer key. You will benefit so much more from the Bible study if you work through the questions on your own, searching your heart, as this is your very personal journey of faith. The answer key is meant to supplement the discussion, or perhaps provide some guidance or insight when needed.

At the end of the book are pages on which to write weekly prayer intentions.

Walking with Purpose™ Website

Please visit our website at www.walkingwithpurpose.com to find additional free content, supplemental materials that compliment our Bible studies, as well as a link to our online store for additional Bible studies, DVDs, book and more!

WWP Scripture Printables of our exclusively designed verse cards that compliment all Bible studies. Available in various sizes, lock screens for phones, and a format that allows you to e-mail them to a friend.

WWP Bible Study Playlists of Lisa's favorite music accompany each Bible study.

WWP Videos of all Connect Coffee Talks by Lisa Brenninkmeyer.

WWP Blog by Lisa Brenninkmeyer you are welcome to come here to find a safe place where the mask can drop and you can be real. Subscribe for updates.

WWP Leadership Development Program
We are here to help you take your leadership to the next level! Through our training, you'll discover insights that help you achieve your leadership potential. You'll be empowered to step out of your comfort zone and experience the rush of serving God with passion and purpose. We want you to know that you are not alone; we offer you encouragement and the tools you need to reach out to a world that desperately needs to experience the love of God.

Links to WWP Social Media

Twitter, Pinterest, Facebook, Instagram

NOTES

Lessons

NOTES

Walking with Purpose is a community of women growing in faith – together! This is where women are gathering. Join us!

www.walkingwithpurpose.com

Lesson 1: Connect Coffee Talk

THE BEAUTY OF A CHILDLIKE FAITH

Based on the teachings of Saint Thérèse of Lisieux, the patron saint of Walking with Purpose

Accompanying talk can be viewed by DVD or digital download purchase or access online at walkingwithpurpose.com/videos.

Three childlike qualities that God desires to see in each of us:

1. Responding to God's Love with Love

"God has revealed his innermost secret: God himself is an eternal exchange of love, Father, Son, and Holy Spirit, and he has destined us to share in that exchange." (CCC 221)

"Love wants to share itself. True love wants to expand its communion. All the hungers we have for love, for union, for happiness are given by God to lead us to Him. The difference between a saint and the greatest sinner is where they go to satisfy that hunger." [1] —Christopher West

Hosea 2:21 (RSV)

Jeremiah 31:3

"As if that were not enough, He invented the Eucharist; a God who makes Himself into bread, a little host, in order to descend onto our lips and into our hearts, to bridge all distance between Himself and us." [2] —Father Jean d'Elbée

---

[1] Christopher West, *An Introduction to the Theology of the Body*, CD (West Chester, PA: Ascension Press, 2008).
[2] Father Jean C. J. d'Elbée, *I Believe in Love* (Manchester, NH: Sophia Institute Press, 2001), 9.

2. Having Confidence in God (He Can Do What You Can't)

Matthew 5:3

Isaiah 57:15

"Jesus, repair what I have done badly; supply for what I have left undone." [3] —Father Jean d'Elbée

"In the evening of my life I shall appear before You with empty hands, for I do not ask You to count my works. All our justices are stained in Your eyes. I want therefore to clothe myself in your own justice and receive from Your love the eternal possession of Yourself." [4] —Saint Thérèse of Lisieux

Isaiah 64:6

2 Corinthians 5:21

Isaiah 53:5

3. Accepting That You're Not in Charge (Surrender)

I desire neither suffering nor death, yet I love both; but it is love alone which attracts me. Now it is abandonment alone that guides me. I have no other compass. My heart is full of the will of Jesus. Ah, if my soul were not already filled with His will, if it had to be filled by the feelings of joy and sadness which follow each other so quickly, it would be a tide of very bitter sorrow. But these alternatives do nothing but brush across my soul. I always remain in a profound peace that nothing can trouble. If the Lord offered me the choice, I would not choose anything: I want nothing but what He wants. It is what He does that I love. I acknowledge that it took me a long time to bring myself to his degree of abandonment. Now I have reached it, for the Lord took me and put me there. [5] —Saint Thérèse of Lisieux

---

[3] Ibid., 59.
[4] Saint Thérèse's Act of Offering, June 9, 1895.
[5] d'Elbée, *I Believe in Love*, 86–7.

Questions for Discussion

1. Have you experienced the difference between white-knuckled striving in the Christian life and the rest that comes from allowing God to do the work through you?

2. "Jesus, repair what I have done badly; supply for what I have left undone." (Father Jean d'Elbée) How does this thought resonate with you as a wife? As a mother? In what area of your life do you most need God to fill in the gap?

3. Most people find surrender difficult. Surrendering to God is the advice given to us in this talk. What characteristics of God help you to surrender? Share your experiences of surrendering to God, or to His will in your life's circumstances.

Lesson 2

WHAT KIND OF A FATHER IS GOD?

Introduction

For some of us, the word *father* brings back memories of warm bear hugs, laughter, and security. For others, *father* triggers complex feelings and painful recollections. The following story was written by a woman who courageously overcame childhood experiences that might otherwise have blocked her ability to receive the love of her heavenly Father. Her hope-filled witness reminds us that we all can find our way to Abba, Father, no matter what our experience of *father* has been.

I grew up in a house with a cinder block fence in front. The fence was four feet high. One day when I was still young enough to be looking up at that fence, my father set me on top of it and told me to jump to him. Little as I was, I knew he would not catch me, and I told him so. He assured me again and again that he would catch me—that I could trust him—that he would never let me fall. We must have argued back and forth for at least five minutes. Finally, I gave in to his request. I still wasn't sure he would catch me, but the hope that he might catch me impelled me to take the risk. I launched myself into the air with arms outstretched and hopes high. Dad stepped aside at the last minute and watched as I hit the grass. Then he leaned down over me, put his finger in my dirt-smeared face, and said, "Don't ever trust anybody!"

Many women have had horrible experiences with the men in their lives—men who should have loved them and protected them, but who hurt them, neglected them, or used them instead. I can relate to these women. You might be wondering how I ever learned to trust my heavenly Father. I wonder the same thing. I think that, through many traumas, the Father hid my heart in His hands. I don't know how He did it, but I know that He did it. I did not escape my youth unscathed, but the Father has made provisions for me to heal and find wholeness. I have walked a journey of discovery about the person of God. Like most people, I projected my earthly father onto our Lord. Little by little, I have come to know God better. Little by little, He has granted me the grace to strip away my misconceptions and replace them with the truth about my heavenly Father's character.

I know that some women cannot imagine a heavenly Father who is safe, loving, and protective of them. Their image of masculinity has been so perverted and disfigured that they are unable to open their hearts to anything masculine. I believe this is one of the reasons that the Father gave us a heavenly mother. Intimacy with the Virgin Mother is a safe and sure way to the heart of God. If past wounds keep you from knowing God's love for you as His beloved daughter, cling to Mary as you study the character of God the Father.

God's desire is for our earthly parents' love to be a taste of the unconditional love He offers us. The *Catechism of the Catholic Church* reflects on how we are to respond when they have failed to love us well:

The language of faith thus draws on the human experience of parents, who are in a way the first representatives of God for man. But this experience also tells us that human parents are fallible and can disfigure the face of fatherhood and motherhood. We ought therefore to recall that God transcends the human distinction between the sexes. He is neither man nor woman: he is God. He also transcends human fatherhood and motherhood, although he is their origin and standard: no one is father as God is Father. (CCC 239)

As you study this lesson, ask the Holy Spirit to use the knowledge in your head to ignite the truth of God's boundless love for you in your heart.

Day One
GOD IS LOVE

Read 1 John 4:16.

1. This Scripture passage tells us that God is _____.

2. First Corinthians 13 tells us what love is. If God is love, then a description of love is a description of God. List the characteristics of love/God (from verses 4–6). Some of the virtues are stated in the negative. Write each virtue as it is described in the Bible, and if it is stated negatively, rewrite it in the positive. For example, *doesn't lie* would be written as is, and then restated as *honest* or *tells the truth*.

A.

B.

C.

D.

E.

F.

G.

H.

I.

3. List the things love/God does (from verses 7–8). Again, write them as they are described in the verses, and then restate them in the positive, where appropriate.

A.

B.

C.

D.

E.

Go back and circle all the qualities and actions of God that you find difficult or impossible to rely on. Write them in the space below:

Quiet your heart and enjoy His presence. . . . Give Him the chance to reveal Himself to you.

When important people in our lives fail to love us well, we often allow those experiences to cloud our impression of who God is and how He loves us. The truth is, God's love is perfect, never failing, and ever enduring. Take some time to reflect on the qualities and actions of God that you find difficult to rely on. Ask Him for the grace to separate your experiences of faulty human love from your beliefs about God's love. Ask Him to reveal Himself to you, and for grace-healed eyes to see Him as He is.

Day Two
GOD IS FAITHFUL

1. Read Isaiah 49:13–16. What do you learn about God's faithfulness from these verses?

2. Read John 3:16–18. Why did God the Father send Jesus into the world? What was His motive? What does this reveal about God the Father's heart?

3. God cares about you personally, so much so that "even the hairs of your head have all been counted" by Him (cf Luke 12:7). According to CCC 27, "The desire for God is written on the human heart because man is created by God and for God; and God never ceases to draw man to himself." Why does God continually draw us to Him? What does God want to give us? See CCC 27 and 30.

These truths are beautifully summarized in this commentary on John 3:16 by Father John Bartunek:

"God loved the world so much that He gave his only Son, so that everyone who believes in him may not be lost but may have eternal life." No hidden agenda, no selfish undertones—pure generosity. This is the heart of God, of the Lord who longs for our friendship. Only when a Christian internalizes this fundamental and overarching motive of God does Christian discipleship really begin to mature. This is Christ's revolution. That disinterested, self-forgetful love has the power to overcome all evil and renew every human heart and the human race as a whole.[6]

Quiet your heart and enjoy His presence. . . . He is FOR YOU.

We question a person's faithfulness to us when we sense that his or her motive in the relationship is self-seeking. When we recognize that someone is really out for him- or herself, we know that a time may come when we end up hurt or betrayed. This is why it's so important for us to recognize that God's desire for us is utterly pure. He is not self-seeking. He has proven on the cross that His love for us is selfless. "No one has greater love than this, to lay down one's life for one's friends." (John 15:13) Take time to reflect on how Jesus proved His faithfulness to us on the cross. Thank Him for resisting the urge to call down legions of angels to rescue Him. Thank Him for staying there until your freedom was won.

---

[6] Father John Bartunek, *The Better Part* (Hamden, CT: Circle Press, 2007), 819.

Day Three
GOD'S HEART IS REVEALED BY JESUS

Oftentimes, we think of God as a harsh father—one who judges and condemns—while we see Jesus as the tender one, the merciful one, the approachable one. But the truth is that every gentle quality we see and experience in Jesus is true of God the Father as well. "He is the reflection of God's glory and the exact imprint of God's very being." (Hebrews 1:3)

1. In the encyclical *Veritatis Splendor*, Saint John Paul II writes, "The light of God's face shines in all its beauty on the countenance of Jesus Christ, 'the image of the invisible God' (*Col* 1:15)."[7] How do the following verses confirm that Jesus is a true representation of who God is? See John 10:30, 10:32, and 12:49–50.

2. What gets in the way of our experiencing an "intimate and vital bond" with God the Father? See CCC 29 and share any insights from your own experience.

3. According to Colossians 1:15–22, who makes forgiveness, healing, and reconciliation with God the Father possible? How was this achieved?

[Jesus] is the image of the invisible God, the firstborn of all creation. For in [Jesus] were created all things in heaven and on earth, the visible and the invisible, whether thrones or dominions or principalities or powers; all things were created by [Jesus] and for [Jesus.] [Jesus] is before all things, and in him all things hold together. [Jesus] is the head of the body, the church. He is the beginning, the firstborn from the dead, that in all things he himself might be preeminent. For in [Jesus] all the fullness [of God] was pleased to dwell, and through [Jesus] to reconcile all things for [God], making peace by the blood of his cross (through

---

[7] John Paul II, *The Splendor of Truth* (Libreria Editrice Vaticana, 1993), 5.

him), whether those on earth or those in heaven. And you who once were alienated and hostile in mind because of evil deeds, [Jesus] has now reconciled in his fleshly body through his death, to present you holy, without blemish, and irreproachable before [God]. (Colossians 1:15–22)

Quiet your heart and enjoy His presence. . . . Your Father wants to embrace you tenderly.

We imagine that God's disapproval of us brings separation, but in reality, whenever there is a chasm between God the Father and us, it is because we have rejected Him. We do not trust Him, and we act apart from His loving guidance. Yet God waits for us, and He thirsts for our friendship. Spend some time contemplating any distance you might be experiencing in your relationship with God. Have you been too distracted by worries and busyness to open your heart to Him? Is there a sin you need to confess? Have you been confused and wrongly assumed that God didn't want to draw close to you? Be assured, He loves you and waits for you. Jesus has made a way for you to go straight to the heart of God. Don't let anything or anyone hold you back from Him.

Day Four
GOD LOVES US AND HATES SIN

Many accounts in the Old Testament teach us that God will not tolerate sin. He lays out serious consequences for those who disobey His commandments. How do we reconcile this image of the "fire and brimstone" God with the loving Father we have been learning about this week?

Imagine you have a little girl who is the love of your life, and one day she disappears. You go to great lengths to find her. You search for days, frantic with despair that you might never see her again. You agonize over the loss of your precious daughter.

When you finally find her, she is dirty and smelly. She is covered with cuts, sores, and bruises. Your little girl is crawling very slowly as she approaches you. She is burning up with fever. What will you do? You will wrap your arms around her, carry her safely home, bathe her carefully and lovingly, treat her wounds, and then take her to the doctor. If medication is prescribed, you will purchase it and give it to her exactly as the doctor instructs, because you want her restored to full and vibrant health. It's not that you don't love her the way she is—you want her to be healthy and whole *because* you love her.

Now try to imagine that when you find your baby girl hurt, infected, and sick with fever, you see a hungry lion stalking her little body, pacing in the shadows, ready to pounce. This is why she used her last bit of strength to crawl away! If you can get the lion to come after you, perhaps she can escape. What will you do?

What does God do?

This filth and sickness is a picture of the sin that infects us. The lion is Satan, and sin is his invitation to approach us. God loves us in the same way we would love a precious daughter. He loves us just as we are, and *because He loves us*, He demands that we be removed from the things that hurt us and can even kill us. He makes a way for us to be clean, healthy, and safe. We can be restored in this way because Jesus got "the lion", Satan, to come after *Him* instead of us. Jesus suffered and died in our place, in order to offer us a way to escape.

God does not reject us because of sin. He rejects sin because of us. It is true that God hates sin. He hates disobedience because it threatens us, it hurts us, it covers us in filth, and it invites the enemy to draw near.

Read Luke 15:11–32.

1. The prodigal son must have been covered in filth when he returned home. At what point did his father run to him?

2. Was the son completely sorry for what he had done to his father?

3. Jesus is telling us that this is what our Father in Heaven is like when we repent. Is this what you expect from your heavenly Father? If not, what do you expect?

Quiet your heart and enjoy His presence. . . . Don't let sin get in the way of living in freedom.

God loves you but hates sin. Why? He hates what sin does to you. Jeremiah 5:25 says, "Your sins have turned back these blessings from you," and there's nothing God wants more than to pour out His blessings on you. God knows that sin separates you from Him, lessens your love for Him, and ultimately enslaves you. "Do you not know that if you present yourself to someone as obedient slaves, you are slaves of the one you obey, either of sin, which leads to death, or of obedience which leads to righteousness?" (Romans 6:16)

God wants His daughters to be free! That means He wants you to run to Him when sin has entangled you. He wants you to ask Him to wash you clean, to heal your wounds, to give you a fresh start. Your experience of freedom is directly proportionate to the degree to which you take confession seriously. What is holding you back? Turn to Him. He will meet you with outstretched arms of mercy.

Day Five
SAINT'S STORY

Saint Scholastica Outdoes Her Brother

If your scale is broken and you don't know it, you'll think you weigh more (or less) than you really do. And then you will adjust your eating and exercise habits inaccurately based on your belief, causing all kinds of unnecessary turbulence in your life. If only the scale had been accurate, or you had known that it was broken!

The *Catechism* (239) tells us that the scale by which we measure God's fatherhood is broken. We tend to judge God the Father based on our fallible human fathers and what they have shown us about fatherhood. In fact, it should be the other way around:

> The language of faith thus draws on the human experience of parents, who are in a way the first representatives of God for man. But this experience also tells us that human parents are fallible and can disfigure the face of fatherhood and motherhood. We ought therefore to recall that God transcends . . . human fatherhood and motherhood, although he is their origin and standard: no one is father as God is Father.

A rightly famous (and true) story about Saint Scholastica illustrates the surprisingly pure goodness and power of God the Father.

Scholastica was Saint Benedict's younger sister. They both grew up in an aristocratic family in central Italy in the late 400s and early 500s. Benedict was given a remarkable vocation: He was the father of Western monasticism. He wrote the rules for monastic life (*Rule of St. Benedict*), which became the basis for monasteries and monastic orders that flourished in the Dark Ages and continue through today. He also founded one of the most famous monasteries in the world, right on the outskirts of Rome: Monte Cassino. (Allied bombers devastated it during World War II, and American benefactors paid for its reconstruction.)

While Benedict was breaking ground on Monte Cassino, Scholastica formed a community of nuns not too far away, using the same rules of life her brother had formulated to create one of the earliest convents in Europe. During the years when their communities were near one another, Benedict visited his sister once a year. At the end of his last visit to her (she died just a little while afterward), she begged him to stay with her that night and continue their lively and deep conversation. He refused, since staying out past sunset would have been a breach of his rules. She insisted (maybe she had a presentiment that she would soon die), but he stubbornly refused. Her eyes flashed, and then she buried her face in her hands as tears welled up in her eyes. Right then, a violent storm broke out. It was so violent that Benedict and his companions couldn't even step out the door; they were forced to continue their visit.

Then occurred a famous little dialogue preserved for history by Pope Gregory the Great, Benedict's biographer. Benedict scolded her, "May God almighty forgive you, sister; what is this that you have done?" Then she raised her head and looked up at him with a mischievous twinkle in her tear-brightened eyes. "I prayed you to stay," she responded, "and you would not hear me; I prayed to almighty God, and He heard me!" Saint Gregory goes on to explain, "No wonder if at that time she were more powerful than he. . . . For according to St. John, 'God is love,' so with good reason she was more powerful who loved more."

When we say that God is Father, too often we think first of the long white beard and the stern, sometimes cold and distant stickler for perfection or enforcer of rules—kind of like Saint Benedict on the night of his last visit to his sister. But the essence of God's fatherhood is found elsewhere. His unlimited power is never, ever divorced from His unlimited goodness and His overflowing, individual love for every single one of His precious daughters.

Do you believe, as Saint Scholastica believed, that God your Father hears your prayers regarding the desires of your heart, and He delights in giving you what is best?

Conclusion

"For you did not receive a spirit of slavery to fall back into fear, but you received a spirit of adoption, through which we cry, 'Abba, Father!'" (Romans 8:15)

"As proof that you are children, God sent the spirit of his Son into our hearts, crying out, 'Abba, Father!' So you are no longer a slave but a child, and if a child then also an heir, through God." (Galatians 4:6–7)

I think we sometimes look at Christianity as the way to make sure that we are forgiven. We're covering our bases so that we are "safe" (as in the baseball kind of "safe"). But when we stop there and go no further, we totally miss out on what God (and Christianity) really offers. What God is truly after is so much more than just forgiving us. He *wants* us. He longs for us to come home to Him, our heavenly Father. Christianity is all about relationship.

When we read the story of the prodigal son, we can mistakenly think it's all about the son finally coming to his senses and asking for forgiveness. But the real focus of the story is the father's heart. It's the picture of the father running to his son the minute he sees him on the horizon. It's about the compassion and joy and mercy that the father is completely thrilled to pour all over his child. And that is exactly how God the Father feels about you.

You are the daughter of a strong, faithful, totally engaged Father, a Father who loves you too much to ignore self-destructive sin in your life, a Father who made sure you had a safe way to get home to Him even before you were born, through Christ's death and resurrection.

Your Father is going to go the distance with you. He knows that you need Him for the long haul. You need to be able to count on Him to stay when everyone else leaves. You'll never stop needing His direction and guidance and parenting. And that's okay, because His love for you is never ending. His arms are always open. You are His beloved. You are safe with Him.

My Resolution

In what specific way will I apply what I learned in this lesson?

Examples:

1. List the characteristics of God the Father you have trouble relying on. Read this list every day and keep your eyes open to see God loving you in these ways.

2. Make a conscious effort to reject any lies or half-truths that might keep you from trusting God with childlike sincerity. Take a risk and count on the truth about who God is—always faithful and true!

My Resolution:

Catechism Clips

CCC 27 The desire for God is written in the human heart, because man is created by God and for God; and God never ceases to draw man to himself. Only in God will he find the truth and happiness he never stops searching for: The dignity of man rests above all on the fact that he is called to communion with God. This invitation to converse with God is addressed to man as soon as he comes into being. For if man exists it is because God has created him through love, and through love continues to hold him in existence. He cannot live fully according to truth unless he freely acknowledges that love and entrusts himself to his creator.

CCC 29 But this "intimate and vital bond of man to God" can be forgotten, overlooked, or even explicitly rejected by man. Such attitudes can have different causes: revolt against evil in the world; religious ignorance or indifference; the cares and riches of this world; the scandal of bad example on the part of believers; currents of thought hostile to religion; finally, that attitude of sinful man which makes him hide from God out of fear and flee his call.

CCC 30 "Let the hearts of those who seek the Lord rejoice." [Psalm 105:3] Although man can forget God or reject him, He never ceases to call every man to seek him, so as to find life and happiness. But this search for God demands of man every effort of intellect, a sound will, "an upright heart," as well as the witness of others who teach him to seek God.

CCC 239 By calling God "Father," the language of faith indicates two main things: that God is the first origin of everything and transcendent authority; and that he is at the same time goodness and loving care for all his children. God's parental tenderness can also be expressed by the image of motherhood, which emphasizes God's immanence, the intimacy between Creator and creature. The language of faith thus draws on the human experience of parents, who are in a way the first representatives of God for man. But this experience also tells us that human parents are fallible and can disfigure the face of fatherhood and motherhood. We ought therefore to recall that God transcends the human distinction between the sexes. He is neither man nor woman: he is God. He also transcends human fatherhood and motherhood, although he is their origin and standard: no one is father as God is Father.

Verse Study

See Appendix 2 for instructions on how to complete a verse study.

Psalm 68:6 (NAB)

1. Verse:

2. Paraphrase:

3. Questions:

4. Cross-references:

5. Personal Applications:

Write the verse on an index card and carry it with you this week.

Lesson 3

WHAT IS THE PURPOSE OF MY LIFE?

Introduction

I've always tended toward saying yes to too many things and overcommitting myself. There are times this has made me feel a little overwhelmed. There have also been times when staying busy has kept me from asking the deeper questions and noticing my inner emptiness. A swirl of activity can delude you into thinking that you're really living, when you're actually just running in the gerbil wheel.

I barreled through high school and college, keeping up my pattern of lots of activities and pursuits. Then I got married, moved to Germany, and everything s-l-o-w-e-d down. My husband traveled Monday through Friday, I didn't have a work permit, didn't have classes to attend, and, horror of horrors, didn't have the Internet or cable. And it got very, very quiet. And the questions started coming. "Why am I here?" "What's the point of my life?" "Is this all there is?"

We can ask these questions when we're wiping noses and making peanut butter and jelly sandwiches. We can ask them from the corner office in a prestigious law firm. We can ask them when we lie in bed with disease or retreat to our rooms with depression.

Feeling lost and purposeless, feeling bland and too busy for passion, feeling stuck in a rut . . . Is this the life God created us for?

No. An emphatic no. *We were created for more.*

Can you sense a restlessness in your soul? A desire for more? A hunger for purpose? Do you feel that somewhere along the way, you lost yourself?

God is pursuing you, and He wants to reveal your part in His story. I say *His* story, because ultimately it is all about Him. When we make it about us, we miss the point.

We end up motivated by ego, or people's opinions, and in the end, we're dissatisfied. But if we'll make *His* story, *His* plan, *His* glory the focus, there's no limit to the good He can do through us. And that means a life of fulfillment and deep satisfaction for us. When our ultimate goal is for Jesus to shine brightly into our world, we are free to dream. We can be bold in our hopes. We can put out into the deep, take risks, and really start living.

Day One
THE PURPOSE WE ALL SHARE

1. Read Philippians 3:7–11. Saint Paul wrote this after describing all the worldly accolades that belonged to him. He considered them all worthless ("I have come to consider everything a loss"), because of what higher good?

   Because of the supreme good of knowing Christ Jesus my Lord.

2. Read 2 Corinthians 5:18–19.

   A. What ministry has God given us and what message has He entrusted to us?

   God has given us reconciliation and entrusted us to sharing the message of reconciliation.

   B. Reconciliation is the act of reestablishing a close relationship between parties. This is exactly what Jesus did for us—He opened the way for us to have a close relationship with our heavenly Father. He now asks us to help reconcile others with Him and with each other. This is one of our core purposes in life. Are there any relationships in your life in which God is asking you to be a peacemaker? *Yes.*

3. Read 2 Corinthians 5:20. How are we described in this verse? In order to be true to this description, how should we interact with others?

Allowing God to work through us we can trust in God to reconcile in His own time and way, to each individual.

Quiet your heart and enjoy His presence. . . . The more you know Him, the more you'll love Him.

Nothing was more important to Saint Paul than knowing Christ. His determined purpose was to continually become more deeply acquainted with Jesus. Every day, he wanted to better know Christ's power and personhood. As he grew in understanding of Jesus, he made it his goal to reflect Jesus to the world. This is God's main purpose for you as well.

To pursue this purpose requires a choice. Worldly accolades satisfy us on some level, but we can't pursue them and also wholeheartedly pursue knowing and reflecting Jesus to the world. We can't do a thousand things well. We have to focus. We have to choose what matters most. These are strong words, but they are true: If we fail to make knowing Christ and becoming more like Him our highest priority, we will have settled for a lesser, shallow existence.

Take some time to prayerfully identify the things that tempt you to take your eyes off your primary purpose (knowing and becoming more like Christ). Is it your reputation? Your desire for comfort? Other goals? Ask God for the grace to put knowing Him and becoming more like Him ahead of all other pursuits.

Day Two
YOUR UNIQUE PURPOSE

Have you ever questioned whether God has a specific plan for your life or if He is too busy with weightier matters to have time for that level of detail concerning you? Be assured—God knows how He wants your life to turn out. His love for you is personal. Your heavenly Father doesn't just look on mankind in general; *He sees you.* He wants you to determinedly pursue the purpose of knowing and becoming more like Jesus, and He wants you to discover the unique contribution He is calling you to make in the world. When He gave out callings and life purposes, *He did not skip you.*

1. What insight do you gain from Psalm 139:13–16 regarding the care God took when He created you?

    Unformed, He created me. Knowing the days shaped ahead of anyone's knowing my existence.

    God's specific plan for your life was put together before you were born, and His plan is *good*. "For I know well the plans I have in mind for you, says the LORD, plans for your welfare, not for woe! Plans to give you a future full of hope!" (Jeremiah 29:11)

2. One of the ways that God reveals your specific calling is by giving you spiritual gifts. Spiritual gifts (also called *charisms*) are given to children of God to help them achieve the purpose they were created for.[8] Read 1 Corinthians 12:1–11 and answer the following questions about spiritual gifts.

    Does God want you to be ignorant of your spiritual gifts? See 1 Corinthians 12:1.

    No, He wants us to become more aware.

    Is the same spiritual gift given to everyone? See 1 Corinthians 12:4–6.

    No, they are individually given.

    Who receives the manifestation of the Spirit? See 1 Corinthians 12:7.

    Each individuals soul will receive the spirit.

    Who is the source of all spiritual gifts? Do you get to choose your spiritual gifts? See 1 Corinthians 12:11. *The Holy Spirit*

    No, it is given to suit you individualy best.

---

[8] For more information about spiritual gifts (charisms), see siena.org (the Catherine of Siena Institute).

3. What are some of the spiritual gifts listed in Scripture? See Romans 12:6–8, 1 Corinthians 12:8–10, and Ephesians 4:11. *Prophecy, Ministry, teaching, exhortation, generosity, leadership, and mercy.*

wisdom, knowledge, faith, healing, mighty deeds, prophecy ext..

Quiet your heart and enjoy His presence . . . . God delights in the way He made you.

apostles, prophets, evangelists, pastors, teachers.

"For we are His handiwork, created in Christ Jesus for the good works that God has prepared in advance, that we should live in them." (Ephesians 2:10)

What a difference it would make if we got that verse into our heads and hearts and really believed it. We could be world changers in our own little corners if we lived as if Ephesians 2:10 were true, instead of spending all the live-long day dwelling on who we are not and what we don't have. It's time to step out and live in the truth that we are God's masterpieces—His handiwork—and He has created us to make a difference. He's placed unique gifts into each one of us, and He wants us to use those gifts to help those around us.

What is holding you back? Are you waiting for the approval of those around you before you live the life God is holding out to you? You don't need it. God offers you courage and strength. He has got your back. Step out. You don't have to be anyone other than the woman God created you to be.

Day Three
HOW TO DISCOVER YOUR CALLING

Before we delve into how to discover your unique calling, it's worth noting that many of us feel so consumed by day-to-day life that we can't imagine adding some enormous *life mission* on top of everything else. It's important to remember that God doesn't want us to live stressed out, overwhelmed, and overcommitted. But He doesn't want us living bored, numb, and empty, either. Somehow we've got to wrestle through the tension that exists when we add to our plates in order to add to the meaning of our lives. It can get a little messy. The alternative—playing it safe and not venturing out into the deep—is the easier option. Living a life that says *yes* to God and His purposes requires bravery. But one day, we'll be standing before God, and we'll have to explain to Him what we've done with the time, spiritual gifts, and other resources He entrusted to us. I don't know about you, but I don't want to tell Him, "I stayed as comfortable as I could. I avoided stress as much as possible. I kept things under control." I want to tell Him that I went *all out.* I want to tell Him I gave it all I had, that sometimes it made me really tired, but that He was worth every bit of it. How about you? Are you ready to start living the life you were created for?

1. What types of service energize you? Can you think of instances when you've shared your time and talent and received positive feedback about the results? *First*

Holy Communion Teacher, VBS teaching and instructing children. Eucharistic minister, speaking + reading aloud.

2. We hear a lot of voices and opinions every day. Because most of us hate to disappoint the people we love, we can spend our whole lives pursuing someone else's dream for us. But living the life that someone else wants you to live (as opposed to the life God is calling you to) will never lead you to your true purpose and calling. Which voices or opinions are pulling you in a certain life direction? List those expectations, and prayerfully consider whether you are pursuing someone else's dream instead of asking God to reveal His plan for you.

God has revealed fruitful plans for me, even in my anxiety to accomplish it.

"Am I now trying to win the approval of human beings, or of God? Or am I trying to please people? If I were still trying to please people, I would not be a servant of Christ." (Galatians 1:10) *This is when anxiety confuses and tries to stop me.*

3. Taking a prayerful look at our "pain files" can be one way we discover our unique callings. If you have struggled through a particular circumstance and have seen the difference God has made during that time, He wants to use that for His purposes. What does God want us to do with the compassion and encouragement He has given us in our times of difficulty? See 2 Corinthians 1:3–4.

He wants us to share that hope and compassion with others, by relating to them.

4. What suffering in the world (and it doesn't have to be far away—it might be in your neighborhood) really wrecks you? What gets you upset enough that you inwardly say, "Something has got to be done about this"?

Mental health because of drugs. Depression in children. Protecting childrens exposure in music, t.v., internet, and from unstable individuals.

"You were made for the place where your real passion meets compassion, because there lies your real purpose." —Ann Voskamp

Quiet your heart and enjoy His presence. . . . Courageously dream with Him of making a difference in the world, together.

Back Sage in His Garden

There isn't a simple formula to discover your unique calling. It's birthed out of time spent in prayerful reflection on your life. Bring before God your holy discontent, your passions, your experiences, your successes, your seasons of pain. Ask God to take what may seem like random events and to thread them together. Ask Him to reveal to you where your real passion meets compassion.

Homeschooling Growing my families faith in the church ministries

Day Four
YOU GET TO DECIDE

God created you with a purpose. He identified specific "works" (things that need to be done to help our hurting world) and He put your name on them. He sees all the things in the world that aren't right, and He wants you to do something about it. He gave you spiritual gifts so you could step out and make a difference. But He won't make you accept the call. He gives you free will. You get to decide what you're going to do with what He's given and revealed.

1. When we discover our spiritual gifts (charisms), it can be tempting to use them to benefit ourselves. But who should ultimately benefit from spiritual gifts? See CCC 799 and 800.

To the good of men and the needs of the world.
For holiness of the entire body of Christ.

"It is a wake-up call, a reminder that we are here for just a moment. How we spend that moment has eternal significance. Wanting more out of life is not about a desire to bring more attention to you. It's about wanting to find a way to do more with your life in a form of worship that ultimately brings more glory to God." —Jennie Allen

2. If we're going to fulfill our callings while reflecting Jesus to the world, what will our attitude need to be? See Matthew 20:26–28.

not to be served but to serve and give our life freely to help many.

3. I'm guessing that you wrote down the right answers to those first two questions. Since they are right in the back of this book, I'll just lay it out here: We are supposed to use our gifts to benefit others and bring glory to God, and we have to have a servant's attitude in order to do it well. So how come so few of us do it? Read John 12:24–25 for insight into this struggle and record your thoughts below.

We are for greater things than those of this world. We must trust in Jesus

Saying yes to God—serving for His sake instead of for our own gain—requires a little death. Do you like feeling in control? You have to let that expectation die, because going where God calls you means life gets messy. Do you like it when everyone approves of you? You have to let that die, because I promise you that doing what God asks of you will mean someone in your life will disapprove of your choice. But my sweet friend, if you will let those things die (and allow all sorts of other little deaths that will come along), you will start to truly *live*.

Don't waste time saying, "I'm just not sure exactly what God is calling me to do. So I'll just sit here and wait until it all becomes clear." Just step out and serve. Meet the need that's right in front of you, without overanalyzing things. The more you serve, the more you'll begin to discover your "sweet spot"—that place where your passion and compassion meet. So what if some of the ways you've served turned out to be a little disastrous? God sees the intention in your heart. He sees the love that motivated you. Regardless of how it all turns out, you've chosen to step out in love. And that is a life well lived.

Quiet your heart and enjoy His presence. . . . Let Him renew your perspective.

Dear Lord,

If I start to feel that what I offer this world is insignificant and pales in comparison to the great things that other people do, help me to remember that I am significant in your eyes. You see the smallest act of love and it matters. Help me to remember that I'm not valued because of my gifts and talents. That is simply what you pour into me so that I can get out in the world and love people the way you love them. I'm valued because you made me; I'm your beloved daughter, and you don't create mistakes.

On the other hand, if I start to get a little impressed with all that I'm doing and the difference I'm making and the way that people around me are thinking I'm pretty fabulous, help me to remember that any good in me comes from you. Help me to never step out in the name of Christian service in my own strength. May everything I do be done through the inner work of your Holy Spirit with the purpose of bringing attention to You, not me.

Day Five
SAINT'S STORY

Saint Rose Philippine Duchesne Gets Her Wish

God's love is not generic. The Church teaches us that every single human being is created directly by God. Even embryos whose material cells are manufactured in petri dishes receive their eternal souls directly from God's hands; no laboratory can concoct a human soul. As a result, every human being has a unique relationship with God. We each know and love Him as *only we can*. In heaven, each of God's children will reflect His infinite magnificence in an entirely unique way. Here on earth, God addresses us by name, and His Providence guides us to be the singular individuals we truly are.

This is why everyone's calling in life is specific; God doesn't send form letters. He converses with each of us personally and guides us *individually*, even as He works in our lives through the great family of the Church. This truth shines brilliantly in the lives of the saints. Each saint's life reflects the specificity of God's action in a remarkably eloquent way.

One such saint was Rose Philippine Duchesne (1769–1852), who came from a well-to-do French family and had everything going for her. As a girl, she channeled her lively temperament and outgoing personality into all kinds of good deeds: visiting the sick and poor, giving alms, playing school. When the French Revolution broke out, she ministered to prisoners waiting their turn at the guillotine; she gathered up orphans, taking care of them and teaching them the *Catechism*.

When she was only eight years old, she heard a homily by a priest who had recently been working in the French missions in America. From that moment on, her deepest desire was to become a missionary herself, and to minister to the Native Americans. More than sixty years would pass before that calling would be fulfilled. At twelve, she told her father that she wanted to join a convent and dedicate her entire life to serving the Sacred Heart. Her father would hear none of it. But she persisted, and in the end she won. Her first obstacle was overcome. The rest of her life would be a series of increasingly larger obstacles, all of them overcome by her gargantuan faith and, most especially, her sheer determination—determination flowing from the Word God had spoken in her heart when she was just a child.

Rose tried to reconvene her convent after the French Revolution (the revolutionaries had dissolved all religious houses), but failed. So she invited another religious order to come take it over. After maturing in her own religious training, she and a couple of other nuns set out for America, where she still longed to be a missionary among the Native Americans. She was forty-nine years old. She fell ill on the trip across the Atlantic and almost died before reaching Louisiana. She fell ill again on the trip up the Mississippi, knocking on death's door for the second time.

When Rose finally reached her mission station, in Saint Charles, Missouri, circumstances continued to stymie her. She had to begin her work with apostolates to the white settlers—schools (including the first free school west of the Mississippi) and orphanages, along with the convents needed to train sisters to run them. She did her best to reach out to the Native Americans in her free time, but she only began working with them full-time when she turned seventy-one and was relieved of some of her administrative duties.

Throughout her years in America she suffered every kind of hardship and difficulty—famine, floods, poverty, sickness, the crudities of paganism (the Native Americans used to bring her fresh scalps as a sign of their reverence)—but her prayer and willpower endured them all, and her missionary activity sowed the seeds of the Catholic Church in the Midwest. Today Rose's name is the first inscribed on the Pioneer Roll of Fame in the Jefferson Memorial Building, in Saint Louis, Missouri.

God had given her a specific call—a personal word to her heart. Her hearing and heeding it, despite mountainous obstacles, changed the world forever.

Do you sense God calling you to action in response to a specific need in the world? Have obstacles caused you to question whether following that call is possible? How does the story of Saint Rose Philippine inspire you to persevere?

As He wills it then it will be done in His time. Anything is possible through Christ our Lord.

Conclusion

"Now I know in part; then I shall know fully, even as I am fully known." (1 Corinthians 13:12)

Your life is not a series of random events. In every circumstance in your life, you are given the opportunity to get to know God a little better, in a unique new way. When you take the time to look for His hand, His mercy, His love, and His healing in every situation, you'll start to gather a greater understanding of God's character and heart. This is your lifelong pursuit—knowing God. One day we'll stand before God, and all those fragments of understanding will come together, and we will "see Him as He is." (1 John 3:2) And it will be incredible!

But that's not all. Although God wants us to live with our eyes on eternity—with our focus on the day we'll meet Him face-to-face—He wants us to use our time here on earth purposefully. He created you for a reason, and He doesn't want you to miss it. One of the reasons this is so important to Him is because He has work that needs to be done in the world—suffering that needs to be relieved, comfort that needs to be given, teaching that needs to be heard, beauty that needs to be created—and He wants to do these things through His people. He wants to use you to fulfill His plan. Another reason this is so important to Him is that He adores you, and wants you to experience the fulfillment and joy that comes from being a part of His story and running the race He created you for. This is *your* race—not your sister's, or your mother's, or your friend's. *Yours.*

Figuring out which race is meant for you is a messy process. It's a matter of always growing in knowledge of who God is, and at the same time, growing in knowledge of who you are. This is different from self-absorbed navel gazing. It's getting to know how you are wired for the purpose of bringing attention to God.

So reflect on the things in life that have been painful. Did God get you through? Did He teach you lessons during that time that you can share with others? Mine that experience. It could be that in the midst of that pain, the seeds of your purpose were planted.

Then take some time to think about the moments in your life when you have never felt so satisfied. Can you remember an experience when you were lost in the joy of the moment, caught up in something greater than you? Make note of that. It may be that your passion was ignited then, and God was calling out to you to keep being His hands and feet in that area of life.

Think about the people who are suffering who just make you ache. Not everyone cares about them the way you do. Could it be that God placed that love and concern in your heart because He aches for them and wants to work through you to help them?

Please don't give up on this journey and just settle for comfortable. And please don't sit on your gifts and your calling because you are afraid that if you step out, you'll be criticized or you'll be too much or not enough. Rise up, and take your place within God's story. Run your race—the race you were created for. Don't miss it. Every moment of your life has meaning. *You* matter. What you offer the world matters. Run your race with your eyes fixed on the finish line, when you'll crash into God's arms, fully known and fully loved.

"The one who called you is faithful and HE WILL DO IT." (1 Thessalonians 5:24)

My Resolution

In what specific way will I apply what I have learned in this lesson?

Examples:

1. I'm going to take some time to prayerfully reflect on my life, listing my passions, pains, and gifts. I'm going to pray about what I think needs to change in the world. I'll ask God to help me to discover the works, the purpose He created me for.

2. I'm going to begin the discernment process to discover my spiritual gifts, or charisms.

3. When I'm tempted to take the easy way out and pursue comfort instead of purpose, I'll ask God for the grace to accept a "little death" in order to experience true growth and fruit.

My Resolution:

Catechism Clips

CCC 799 Whether extraordinary or simple and humble, charisms are graces of the Holy Spirit which directly or indirectly benefit the Church, ordered as they are to her building up, to the good of men, and to the needs of the world.

CCC 800 Charisms are to be accepted with gratitude by the person who receives them and by all members of the Church as well. They are a wonderfully rich grace for the apostolic vitality and for the holiness of the entire Body of Christ, provided they really are genuine gifts of the Holy Spirit and are used in full conformity with authentic promptings of this same Spirit, that is, in keeping with charity, the true measure of all charisms.

Verse Study

See Appendix 2 for instructions on how to complete a verse study.

Jeremiah 9:23 (NAB)

1. Verse:

2. Paraphrase:

3. Questions:

4. Cross-references:

5. Personal Applications:

Write the verse on an index card and carry it with you this week.

Lesson 4

HOW DOES GOD DEFINE BEAUTY?

Introduction

Beauty is a hot topic. Who among us doesn't want to be beautiful? Sadly, many of us have a faulty definition of beauty and are caught up in the endless and expensive pursuit of physical perfection. Some of us know that true beauty has more to do with what's inside than what's outside, yet we still feel our sense of worth rises and falls depending on what we look like.

In our culture, beauty has become a two-dimensional billboard: an advertisement for ME. As long as we are satisfied with a self-centered, inwardly focused life, there isn't a problem with this arrangement. Life in the superficial lane can keep us busy (it takes time to perfect a selfie that barely shows your arm holding the camera), but it leaves us feeling empty and dissatisfied.

We were made for more. We have been wired to live lives of significance, and when we are in tune with the reason we were created, we'll inevitably want our lives to count and to be centered not on ourselves, but on the Lord. We want to shine His light into darkness instead of feeling depressed that we don't measure up.

One modern example of true beauty is Saint Teresa of Calcutta. Have you ever seen a picture of her bright and beaming smile? What do you think of when you see this? *Wow! When was the last time that woman exfoliated? She could really use a chemical peel!* Of Bible study these comments are absurd—but *why* are they absurd? We are talking about the face that brought the love of Christ into the slums and filthy holes of the poorest of the poor. Her wrinkled, knotted hands nursed the dying, cradled the orphans, and pointed the way to the heart of Christ. She had real inner beauty. Her beauty came from her abiding connection to Christ. When we look at Saint Teresa of Calcutta, we don't see a shriveled little old woman. We see power, we see audacity, we see love; we see Christ. Saint Teresa of Calcutta loved Jesus extravagantly, and as she kept her gaze on Him, *His* beauty and glory emanated from her. Father Michael van der Peet, who preached at least one retreat for the Missionaries of Charity, said of her:

Whenever I met Mother, all self-consciousness left me. I felt right away at ease: she radiated peace and joy, even when she shared with me the darkness in her spiritual life. I was often amazed that someone who lived so much face to face with suffering people and went through a dark night herself, still could smile and make you feel happy. . . . I believe that I can say that I felt in God's presence, in the presence of truth and love . . . yet at the same time . . . she was one of the most down-to-earth persons I have ever met.[9]

When we describe someone as "down-to-earth," we generally mean that she is genuine. She is authentic. She isn't trying to act like or look like someone she is not. Saint Teresa of Calcutta accepted herself (wrinkles and all) and just got on with the business of loving radically. She made her life sacred and holy by offering herself back to God to do with as He pleased.

Fine, you say, *but I am no Saint Teresa of Calcutta*. Well, neither am I. But we are God's precious daughters just the same. He wants to shine through us as well. He wants us to be confident and radiant because we are full to overflowing with His tender love and joy. He does not want our self-worth to rise and fall with clear skin or bad hair days.

When we shift our focus away from ourselves and look outward—toward God and others—we can retire from the rat race of seeking external perfection. We will care for our bodies with a sense of gratitude for His wonderful gift to us, and we will stop obsessing about appearances. Like Saint Teresa of Calcutta's, our beauty will shine forth as the result of a heart lovingly surrendered to God and poured out to others in His service and for His glory.

Day One
THE MOST PRECIOUS PART OF YOU

1. According to CCC 363, what is the most valuable part of you?

God's Image inside us. Our soul

---

[9] Mother Teresa, *Mother Teresa: Come Be My Light* (New York: Doubleday Religion, 2007), 269.

2. When God looks at you, how does His perspective differ from that of most people? See 1 Samuel 16:7.

God looks within us, past what is only skin deep.

3. What is the biblical perspective on the visible signs of aging? See Proverbs 16:31 and 2 Corinthians 4:16.

Grey hair is our crown of glory God transforms us within as our body's age we become more valuble inside.

Quiet your heart and enjoy His presence. . . . Ask Him to renew you from the inside out.

Our souls can become more and more beautiful even while our bodies are "moving backward" with age. But this doesn't happen automatically. Only women who turn their hearts over to the Lord experience this inner renewal. All too often, our hearts are surrounded by walls of bitterness and unforgiveness. Our souls can grow hard from unconfessed sin. The good news: God is in the business of softening our hearts. He can breathe new life into hearts that have long felt dead. Have you been so hurt that you wonder if you can ever love again? Has betrayal caused you to vow that you will never rely on another person besides yourself? Has your self-sufficiency caused you to close you heart off to your Healer? Has unconfessed sin built a wall around your heart? Ask God to break down the walls, renewing you from the inside out.

Day Two
CARE FOR IT WITHOUT OBSESSING ABOUT IT

1. Our soul is the most valuable part of who we are, but we aren't only made up of a soul. "The human person, created in the image of God, is a being at once corporeal and spiritual." (CCC 362) Our bodies matter, and we have to make peace with them. According to CCC 364, how are we to regard our bodies? Do you find this easy to do?

as good and it will be raised up on the last day.

no, but I'm trying more as I age. Its keep transforming to care for it. instead of dwell stuck in it

When God created man, He "saw all that he had made, and it was very good." (Genesis 1:31) Beauty is defined by God because He created it. Our culture has hijacked the definition of beauty and twisted it into something purely external, but that doesn't change its true definition.

We are to "regard our bodies as good." Even as we read that sentence, most of us start to think about all the aspects of our bodies that we *don't* think are good. This is because we dissect our body parts, and measure each one against the cultural ideal. And this is *messed up*. This is not the way that God wants us to analyze our bodies' worth. He wants our focus to be renewed, and for us to see that He's given each one of us a body not so that we can gain attention or admiration. He's given it to us so that we can love. Bags under your eyes from staying up late listening to a friend in need, a saggy stomach from pregnancy, wrinkled hands from years of service—all these things are beautiful in His eyes.

2. Regarding our bodies as gifts given to us by God should cause us to take care of them. That being said, caring for our bodies is not the same as obsessing about our bodies. "For while bodily training is of some value, godliness is of value in every way, as it holds promise for the present life and also for the life to come." (1 Timothy 4:8) Staying in shape *spiritually* should be our highest priority.

We can step toward a balanced approach to this by evaluating the amount of time, effort, and money we spend developing outer and inner beauty. In the following exercise, fill in the details of your beauty routine.

Beauty Routine

Outer Beauty **Daily Routine**	**Inner Beauty** **Daily Routine**
Morning *wash face* *brush teeth* *get ready for day* Time Spent: *30 min*	Morning *quiet time to myself* Time Spent: *1 hour*
Evening *shower* *brush/floss* *ready for bed* Time Spent:	Evening *bible study or formal movie* Time Spent:

Monthly Routine

Jacuzzi

Time Spent: *1 hour*

Money spent per month:

HOA Fee

Monthly Routine

prayer group

Time Spent: *6 hours*

Money spent per month:

100.00

fuel, course book food.

3. What changes can you make to shift toward a focus on inner beauty?

For fun, watch this YouTube video of a model being prepared for a photo shoot. It is eye-opening! Go to www.youtube.com. Type **Dove Ad: The Evolution of Beauty** in the search box.

Clearly, if we're comparing ourselves to the magazine models, we're going to come up short and feel dissatisfied. It's time to stop. As Audrey Hepburn said, "I believe that happy girls are the prettiest girls." We'll grow in happiness and contentment if we accept ourselves as we are, recognizing that God designed us, and He doesn't make mistakes.

Quiet your heart and enjoy His presence. . . . The Creator of Beauty delights when you turn your face toward Him.

"Your adornment must not be merely external—braiding the hair, and wearing gold jewelry, or putting on dresses; but let it be the hidden person of the heart, with the imperishable quality of a gentle and quiet spirit, which is precious in the sight of God." (1 Peter 3:3–4)

The Bible doesn't condemn us for wearing jewelry and making an effort to look nice, and it doesn't hold up frumpiness as a virtue. But God wants us to be clear on what matters most, and that is the state of our hearts. Our highest priority should be inner beauty, not outer appearance. Spend some time thanking God for the way He made your body. Think about how your body serves you as you step out and love others. Ask God to help you to pursue health, balance, and true beauty instead of getting caught up in our culture's faulty definition of what is lovely and admirable.

Day Three
INNER BEAUTY CHECKUP

The following verses describe two aspects of inner beauty. After you read each one, write down what you've learned.

1. Beauty in thought:

   Philippians 4:8

   (remain in the mindset of) Calls us to dwell in things that are praiseworthy

   2 Corinthians 10:3–5

   the Holy Spirit is evidence that they did have a relationship with God knowledge of God through every thought

   Luke 6:37

   forgiveness / no judgments

2. Beauty in speech:

   James 1:19

   listen to others, slow to speak

   James 1:26

   Religious but do not have self control in what you say

   Ephesians 4:29

   no corrupt communication minister grace

3. With which of these disciplines do you have the most trouble? Write out that verse in the space below.

   No foul language should come out of your mouths, but only such as is good for needed edification, that it may impart grace to those who hear.

Quiet your heart and enjoy His presence. . . . Allow His words to take root in your heart.

"Set a guard over my mouth, O Lord; keep watch over the door of my lips." (Psalm 141:3)

Without God's help, we're going to find it impossible to speak in a way that is consistently filled with grace. Thankfully, God is able to do the impossible. He can help us build others up with our words instead of tearing them down.

But God wants to go even deeper than that. He doesn't just care about what comes out of our mouths. He is concerned with what's in our heads and hearts. He wants our thoughts and attitudes to reflect Jesus. Our prayer time is His opportunity to do a makeover on our souls—cleansing us of our negative thoughts, pulling up roots of bitterness, uncovering critical spirits, and helping us break free from the bondage of un-forgiveness.

God is a gentleman. He'll only help us in these ways if we invite Him to. Can you ask Him to help you in your area of struggle?

Day Four
GOD'S DESIRE FOR YOU

Throughout history and continuing today, women have been objectified and valued for their sensuality. Too many of us have been used for pleasure and then discarded. We're continually sold the message, "If you've got it, flaunt it." The attention feels good for a little while because there is a part of all of us that wants to be desired.

God desires you, but not in a sensual way. His passion for you is totally pure. Read the following verses, and note the difference between the way God relates to you and our lust-saturated culture's approach.

1. Isaiah 61:10: "I rejoice heartily in the LORD, in my God is the joy of my soul; For he has clothed me with a robe of salvation, and wrapped me in a mantle of justice, Like a bridegroom adorned with a diadem, like a bride bedecked with her jewels."

2. Ephesians 5:25–27: "Husbands, love your wives even as Christ loved the church and handed himself over for her to sanctify her, cleansing her by the bath of water with the word, that he might present to himself the church in splendor, without spot or wrinkle or any such thing, that she might be holy and without blemish."

3. Revelation 19:7–8: "Let us rejoice and exult and give him the glory, for the marriage of the Lamb has come, and his Bride has made herself ready; it was granted her to be clothed with fine linen, bright and pure—for the fine linen is the righteous deeds of the saints."

Quiet your heart and enjoy His presence. . . . He is enthralled by your beauty.

As your heavenly Father looks at you, He sees your heart of love and all the ways in which you step out as His hands and feet in our hurting world. He sees you dressed in Christ's robe of salvation. He sees your virtue and your desire to please Him. And He smiles, because He is so pleased with what He has made. Don't hide your beauty. "You are the light of the world. A city set on a mountain cannot be hidden. Nor do they light a lamp and then put it under a bushel basket; it is set on a lampstand, where it gives light to all in the house. Just so, your light must shine before others that they may see your good deeds and glorify your Father in heaven." (Matthew 5:14–16)

Day Five
SAINT'S STORY

Saint Agnes of Rome

Agnes was a beautiful girl, both inside and out. She was decorous and sweet, with the grace of a girl just entering the first flush of womanhood. But her heart was lost in another beauty, for the Lord had already enchanted her with His goodness and purity. She completely committed herself to the Lord, declaring that he would be her only spouse.

Agnes was unconscious of the spell that her beauty had cast on the son of the prefect of Rome. This young man saw her and decided he must have her. Such is the lowliest kind of human love: it does not consider the good of the beloved nor of surrender and giving, but rather it is selfish, consumed with thoughts of possessing, enjoying, and deflowering.

The son approached Agnes to ask for her hand in marriage, but she refused. Smitten all the more, he returned within the week laden with jewels and treasures to convince her to say yes. "I will make you lovely like a queen," he said, "and no woman will compare with you." Agnes was not convinced. She knew that her soul was already adorned with precious jewels far greater in value than those of any earthly prince, for the King of Heaven and Earth had already chosen her for His own.

However, this was not the end of the discussion. When his powerful father heard that his son was lovesick and inconsolable, he took matters into his own hands. Once again, Agnes was offered jewels and cajoling promises—this time from the father. And when she declined his offer again, she received threats. Christians were already suffering from religious persecution in Rome, and when Agnes refused, she knew her life was in danger. But nothing weakened Agnes' resolve. Her strength had been forged in prayer and she was prepared.

After hearing that not only had this girl refused his son, but she was also a Christian, the prefect came raging like the devil and gave Agnes a choice: she would denounce Christianity and worship the pagan gods in the temple, or be thrown into a brothel to be dishonored and defiled. Agnes chose the brothel. She was stripped of her clothing and paraded naked through the street. Miraculously, her hair grew and covered her naked body like a golden curtain, preserving her from shame. In the brothel, an angel appeared to her and surrounded her with a bright, clear light. She was surrounded by the Lord's protection, praying all the while.

One by one, men entered the room. But when they saw the light around her, they dared not touch her. The son of the prefect, however, was not one to be stopped by the light. He approached Agnes, but he never reached her, falling dead in the room. For these miraculous occurrences, the Romans were convinced she was a witch, and decided to burn Agnes at the stake. They prepared the fire to throw her in, but she was unharmed in the flames. The soldiers resorted to killing her with one thrust of the sword. Her earthly life was ended and her soul flew to be with the Lord in heaven.

There, the Lord clothed her richly in the white garment of perpetual virginity and took her to Himself. There, in the eyes of the Lord, Agnes saw the beauty He had placed in her. This is the beauty the Lord has prepared for His faithful ones: an undying glory of light—the effulgence of all the virtues—whose true radiance is seen at last through heaven's eyes.

Why pursue earthly beauty, which will soon slip through your fingers, when there is a much greater beauty that awaits you in the love that you have given to your Lord? Each woman has her calling. The demands of love are unique for each. Some love the Lord in their virginity. Others love Him in a holy marriage with an earthly husband, raising children as Our Lady raised Jesus. Motherhood is a crown of beauty for the woman who loves well.

Mothers understand sacrifice; they understand the love that is a free gift, willing to give without receiving anything in return. A mother's love is pure, intuitive, gentle, and powerful. It can quench fires before they ignite in the home. Her love can save her children from spiritual death. A mother and a wife is the light of her home, the joyful voice that greets her husband and children every morning, the gentle caress on their days of exhaustion or discouragement. She is balm, sweetness, and strength for those she loves.

Persevere in loving the Lord and the lambs He has entrusted to you, and one day you will see the crown of glory that awaits you.

In what way have you experienced the beauty that comes from a mother's love? It could be an example from your mother, or someone who has been like a mother to you. *From my Children, my grandmother, and the Blessed Mother.*

Conclusion

"They looked to Him and were radiant, and their faces will never be ashamed." (Psalm 34:5)

A truly beautiful woman radiates love and humility because she is obedient to Christ. Far from being merely decorative, she has a role to play in the great adventure of salvation history. Saint Teresa of Calcutta knew this, and recognized that the beauty God had created in her was meant to be shared with others. She made her life sacred and holy by offering herself back to God to do with as He pleased. God's inner beauty salon is the school of loving obedience. Saint Teresa of Calcutta vowed never to say no to God. And look what God did! She was like a piece of stained glass designed by Him. She was fitted into the Church in exactly the place the Lord had constructed for her. The light, love, and beauty of God poured through her to the poorest of the poor, and to us as well.

Every woman has a beauty to share, and the world desperately longs for it to be seen. There's nothing lovelier than a woman who knows that God created her for a purpose, that she has something to offer, and that her strength, her ability to nurture, her wisdom, and her influence are needed. A woman like this inspires others to greatness, filling our communities with hope and our homes with grace.

You are God's sacred art, a beautiful stained-glass window designed by Him. God has prepared a place for you. He is ready to fill your life with light, love, and beauty. What remains is for you to offer yourself to Him—imperfections and all. As Saint John Paul II used to say, "Open wide the doors of your heart to Christ."

My Resolution

In what specific way will I apply what I have learned in this lesson?

Examples:

1. I resolve to live out Philippians 4:8 by choosing to thank God every day for the way He created me. I'll be specific, choosing three traits I am grateful for. *Creativity   leadership*

2. I resolve to carve out an extra hour this week for an "inner beauty treatment." This may be an extra hour of reading the Bible or a spiritual book, or an hour of adoration. *self care*

3. As I get dressed and ready for the day, I will be aware of my thoughts. Whom am I prepping to please? Am I criticizing myself? I will stop. Instead, I will thank God for His good gifts regarding my appearance. I will ask Him to allow me to see myself through His eyes. I will prepare myself for this day with tender loving care because this is what the Lord wants for me.

My Resolution: *I will see the Fathers love in all my day*

Catechism Clips

CCC 362 The human person, created in the image of God, is a being at once corporeal and spiritual. The biblical account expresses this reality in symbolic language when it affirms that "then the Lord God formed man of dust from the ground, and reathed into his nostrils the breath of life; and man became a living being." [Genesis 2:7] Man, whole and entire, is therefore willed by God.

CCC 363 In Sacred Scripture the term "soul" often refers to human life or the entire human person. But "soul" also refers to the innermost aspect of man, that which is of greatest value in him, that by which he is most especially in God's image: "soul" signifies the spiritual principle in man.

CCC 364 The human body shares in the dignity of "the image of God": it is a human body precisely because it is animated by a spiritual soul, and it is the whole human person that is intended to become, in the body of Christ, a temple of the Spirit:

Man, though made of body and soul, is a unity. Through his very bodily condition he sums up in himself the elements of the material world. Through him they are thus brought to their highest perfection and can raise their voice in praise freely given to the Creator. For this reason man may not despise his bodily life. Rather he is obliged to regard his body as good and to hold it in honor since God has created it and will raise it up on the last day.

Verse Study

See Appendix 2 for instructions on how to complete a verse study.

Use the verse that you wrote down for Day Three, Question 3. Memorizing it will allow the Holy Spirit to bring it to your mind just when you need a reminder!

1.   Verse:

2.   Paraphrase:

3.   Questions:

4.   Cross-references:

5.   Personal Applications:

Write the verse on an index card and carry it with you this week.

No program near you? No problem...it's easy to start your own group in your parish or at home and we will walk with you every step of the way. Find out more:

www.walkingwithpurpose.com

Lesson 5

HOW DO I WORK AT FORGIVING MYSELF AND OTHERS?

Introduction

"Forgiveness also bears witness that, in our world, love is stronger than sin." (CCC 2844)

"To err is human; to forgive, divine." This is an undeniable bit of wisdom. Yet when we've been wounded, we are probably feeling all too human. Still, Jesus requires forgiveness of us, and we know God grants the grace to accomplish what He commands. We know we must forgive, but often we don't know how. Perhaps we don't even know what forgiveness is! Let's look at some basic principles of forgiveness so that we may discern what God is really asking when He tells us He will forgive us just as we forgive others.

It is often easier to understand what something is when we take the time to learn what it is not:

- Forgiveness is not forgetting or denying that a wrong was done to you.
- Forgiveness is not condoning or making excuses for the wrongdoer.
- Forgiveness is not a superior person granting pardon to an inferior person.
- Forgiveness does not require a return to a dangerous situation or relationship.

Now that we have a sense of what forgiveness is not, let's consider what it is. Simply put, forgiving someone means that you will not try this person in the courtroom of your own heart. You cancel his or her spiritual debt to you, for having wounded you. True forgiveness means releasing this person to stand before the just Judge: the Lord.

Forgiveness is a choice, a decision—and one we may have to make repeatedly. Just as love is an act of our will and is not based on our emotions, so, too, is forgiveness. The decision to forgive is often not a onetime event; it is a process. We choose to walk forward with our hand in the Lord's, depending on His grace and wisdom to strengthen our will to forgive. If we allow the Lord a free hand to work in us through pain and obedience, suffering will carve out more space for His sweet presence in our hearts. Our prayer lives will deepen. We will grow more like our Lord and enjoy a fuller, richer fellowship with Him and everyone else in our lives!

Day One
FORGIVEN AS WE FORGIVE

Read Matthew 6:7–15.

1. The central message of the Our Father is the importance of forgiveness. What important point did Jesus make about forgiveness in this passage? How do we know that He really wanted to drive this point home? See also CCC 2838.

2. According to CCC 2840, what will prevent Christ's outpouring of mercy from penetrating our hearts? Why? What opens our hearts to His grace?

3. Read this commentary from *The Better Part*, by Father John Bartunek, and answer the questions that follow.

> Forgiveness requires humility. . . . Basically, humility means recognizing that you are not God, and when we refuse to forgive someone, we are forgetting precisely that. A refusal to forgive involves passing judgment on the offender. But to pass judgment on another person is to put oneself in God's place. Only God can see the whole interior world of a human being; only God can see into the secret recesses of the human heart. And so, only God has the right to pass judgment. (This same reasoning applies to forgiving yourself; a refusal to forgive yourself comes, ultimately, from arrogance. We find it hard to forgive ourselves if we think we are so perfect that we, unlike

normal human beings, are beyond the possibility of falling short, failing or sinning—it indicates a shortage of healthy humility.)

So those who refuse to forgive are acting like God, elevating themselves above their offender. But acting like God inhibits them from recognizing their true dependence on God and their own need for his forgiveness—the throne of judgment only has enough room for one judge at a time, either oneself or God. This attitude, then, simply ousts God, shutting the door on him. And so the merciful, forgiving God is left standing outside in the cold, unable to bring us his forgiveness.

The tragedy of this dilemma is that every human soul needs to experience God's forgiveness in order to be at peace. And so, the unforgiving person ends up destroying himself in his self-righteous attempt to destroy his neighbor.[10]

A. How does withholding forgiveness demonstrate a lack of humility before God?

B. How does withholding forgiveness from yourself demonstrate a lack of humility before the Lord?

4. Do you believe that forgiving others, asking for forgiveness, and receiving forgiveness from God is the starting point for solving problems? Why or why not?

---

[10] Bartunek, *The Better Part*, 105.

Quiet your heart and enjoy His presence. . . . Open your heart to the healing balm of His forgiveness.

Dear Lord,

I am so grateful that there is no limit to your forgiveness. Sometimes I hesitate to ask for it because I feel like what I've done is just too awful. Holy Spirit, please continue to whisper the truth into my heart that no sin is beyond the reach of Your mercy. Sometimes I don't ask for forgiveness because I'm busy comparing myself to others and am preoccupied by their need for forgiveness. Please help me to grow in humility, always making my own sin and shortcomings the starting point—not theirs. And then there's the issue of me forgiving others. Sometimes I can offer this easily, and then other times it's as if I've hit a brick wall, and I simply cannot do it. At those moments, please remind me that "with God, all things are possible." (Matthew 19:26) Help me to not rest until I wrestle through this with You. I desperately need Your forgiveness, and so I desperately need to forgive others. Heal my hurts, help me to look at others with grace-healed eyes, and give me the strength to offer others the forgiveness I have received from You.

Day Two
THE ISSUE OF EXCUSES

In C. S. Lewis' "Essay on Forgiveness," he unpacks how excuses impact the way in which we ask for forgiveness and our difficulty in offering it:

> The trouble is that what we call "asking God's forgiveness" very often really consists in asking God to accept our excuses. What leads us into this mistake is the fact that there usually is some amount of excuse, some "extenuating circumstances." We are so very anxious to point these things out to God (and to ourselves) that we are apt to forget the very important thing; that is, the bit left over, the bit which excuses don't cover, the bit which is inexcusable but not, thank God, unforgivable. And if we forget this, we shall go away imagining that we have repented and been forgiven when all that has really happened is that we have satisfied ourselves with our own excuses. They may be very bad excuses; we are all too easily satisfied about ourselves. . . .

> In our own case we accept excuses too easily, in other people's we do not accept them easily enough. As regards my own sins it is a safe bet (though not a certainty) that the excuses are not really so good as I think; as regards other men's sins against me it is a safe bet (though not a certainty) that the excuses are better than I think. One must therefore begin by attending to everything which may show that the other man was not so much to blame as we thought.

But even if he is absolutely fully to blame we still have to forgive him; and even if ninety-nine percent of his apparent guilt can be explained away by really good excuses, the problem of forgiveness begins with the one percent of guilt that is left over.[11]

1. Do Lewis' words ring true to you? Does his perspective make you look at forgiveness differently?

2. Read Matthew 7:1–5. Can you think of a time in your life when you had a plank in your eye, but the splinter in your brother's eye seemed the larger of the two issues?

3. Matthew 7:1 tells us that we are not to judge. Does this mean that we aren't allowed to form opinions about the right and wrong of actions?

We are to be wise students of human nature. Each time we encounter our own failings or those of someone else, we can learn something. When we choose to refrain from judging someone, that doesn't mean we turn around and offer blind trust. We need to read situations, and make wise decisions. Refraining from judging and offering forgiveness doesn't mean that we deny reality and put ourselves in unsafe or unhealthy situations. It doesn't mean that we act as if the sin never happened. It does mean that we watch what we say about it to others, we monitor our thoughts about the person involved, and we nip resentment in the bud by remembering our own need for mercy.

---

[11] C. S. Lewis, "Essay on Forgiveness" (New York: Macmillian Publishing Company, 1960).

Quiet your heart and enjoy His presence. . . . He has the wisdom to help you discern the truth in every situation.

Dear Lord,

You know everything. You know my motives, my desire to do the right thing, and the obstacles I face. You see every detail. Help me to remember that only you can see that level of detail in the lives of the people around me. I think I've got the whole picture, and I rarely actually do. Help me to try to see things from others' perspectives, and to be generous in my assessment of the obstacles they face as they go through life. May I be magnanimous with my good opinion instead of being characterized by a critical spirit. Everyone I meet is fighting some kind of a battle. Help me to be gentle with the people you place in my path- —in my actions, words, and attitudes.

Day Three
THE BATTLE TO FORGIVE

The following is an excerpt from a blog post written by a woman who has walked the road of forgiving a spouse for an affair. She knows from experience how easily resentment and un-forgiveness can ruin us from within. She writes to all of us who may be stuck in the quicksand of anger and hurt.

> This anger you keep just under the surface of your heart is a part of you. You wouldn't know who you were without it. Your anger allows you to be in control. **Living in the hurt of the past allows you to brace yourself to deal with the disappointments and hurt in the future. You find your identity in your resentment.**
>
> If that's the case, the truth is that there is a part of your heart you are not just withholding from the person you can't forgive. You are withholding that part of your heart from God. And God longs to heal you, to free you, to form you and shape you into the person you were created to be. . . .
>
> In reality, you are terrified that if you forgive, you will be admitting defeat. If you forgive, they win. **But forgiveness doesn't excuse their behavior. Forgiveness prevents their behavior from destroying your heart.** Forgiveness prevents forfeiting your future by [keeping you from] living in your past. Forgiveness prepares you to move from ordinary to extraordinary.

When you forgive, the person who hurt you doesn't win—Christ wins. He wins another part of your heart.[12]

1. Is there a part of your heart that you have been withholding from God because of fear of getting hurt again? Is your fear of potential pain and disappointment holding you back from being shaped into the person you were created to be?

2. Once we make the decision to forgive, we'll find that a battle is being waged in our minds and hearts. Old memories of the hurt will come back. Things will happen that remind us of what occurred, and it will trigger all the same emotions to come rushing back. Our imagination will kick in and we'll think of all sorts of what-ifs, and we'll be tempted to read into situations, assuming the worst. So how do we respond? Read the following verses for some tips.

   Philippians 4:8

   Matthew 5:44

   1 Corinthians 10:13

   Matthew 18:21–22

3. It isn't in our power not to feel or to forget an offense, but a heart that offers itself to the Holy Spirit experiences something incredible. What is it? See CCC 2843

---

[12] Trisha Davis, "Beyond Ordinary Forgiveness," In Courage (blog), April 10, 2013, http://www.incourage.me/2013/04/beyond-ordinary-forgiveness.html.

Quiet your heart and enjoy His presence. . . . Only He can turn the injury into compassion and the hurt into intercession.

"And I am sure of this, that he who began a good work in you will bring it to completion at the day of Jesus Christ." (Philippians 1:6)

Don't be discouraged by the long road that forgiveness requires. It does take time, and time doesn't heal all wounds. God does, though, if we let Him. He is the One who placed the desire for healing within your heart. He is the One who gives the strength to offer forgiveness when it isn't deserved. And He is the one who gets to work in our hearts and transforms the dead, aching, hurt places into places of hope. When doubts, fears, and resentments rear their heads, run to Jesus. Ask Him to share His forgiving heart with you. Ask Him to fill you with the mercy He drew on when He forgave those crucifying Him. He will be faithful to you. He will not leave you stranded. He will provide all you need to forgive—not just once, but time and time again.

Day Four
FORGIVING OUR ENEMIES

Read Appendix 3: Corrie ten Boom Article

1. How capable of forgiveness did Corrie ten Boom feel when the Ravensbrück guard put out his hand to her? How was she able to do this? Describe her part and God's part in the process.

2. Read CCC 2844 and put it in your own words below.

3. Do you see evidence of the ways in which withholding forgiveness impacts your relationship with other people, not just the person you need to forgive? Has a root of bitterness and anger lodged in your heart? Whom do you need to forgive? Write a prayer to the Lord, telling Him honestly how you feel, and asking Him to give you the strength to take the first step toward healing.

Quiet your heart and enjoy His presence. . . . Let His mercy fill every corner of your heart.

Forgiving what feels unforgivable—we simply cannot do it in our own strength. But with God, all things are possible. Jesus, who was able to forgive those crucifying Him even as He experienced indescribable pain, offers His own merciful heart to us. Once we make the decision to forgive, when we take the first step, when we say the words or write the letter or lift the hand, He gives us what we need to make it genuine. He then is free to heal us, to bring us the freedom we long for. Truly, divine love *is stronger than sin. And it is ours for the asking. Can you ask the Lord for it? Can you ask Him for what you lack? He will give you the courage you need to take the first step. Go to Him with your empty, hurting, angry heart. Ask Him for what you need. Don't put it off. He is waiting for you, right now.*

Day Five
SAINT'S STORY

Saint Maria Goretti

Maria Goretti was born into poverty, made infinitely worse when her father died from malaria. She and her family were forced to leave their home while her mother looked for work in the service of other farmers.

They ended up sharing a small house with another family, which included a young man named Alessandro. On many occasions, Alessandro made sexual advances to young Maria, which she vehemently refused. One afternoon, he grabbed Maria and tried to force himself on her. Maria fought him off and tried to reason with him. "Alessandro, God does not wish it, it is a mortal sin! If you do this, you will go to hell!" He became violently angry, stabbing Maria numerous times all over her body and left her to die.

As she lay dying, Maria entrusted herself to God and the Blessed Virgin Mary; she prayed to be found, prayed for Alessandro, prayed for her mother, and prayed for God to accept her soul. Her fleshed was ravaged, but her heart was intact. It was not only her virginity that was spared that day, but also her purity of heart, which even then chose not to hate. By the grace of God, Maria chose to forgive.

It is always a choice to forgive. It is not a question of emotions, but a decision of the heart, that deepest center where we decide who we want to be, how we want to live, and how we want to die. Jesus shows us the way; it is our choice to walk it.

Forgiveness is also an act of faith. Even when Maria's body was in the hands of her enemy, she trusted that her heart and her soul were safe in the hands of God. She knew that there is no snatching away from Him. She trusted that no matter what happened, her Good Shepherd would never abandon her. The disease of resentment did not infect Maria because she did not let it in. She kept her soul virgin, free of vengeance, nourished with grace and love, like a lamb grazing in fields of green.

After her death, Maria appeared to Alessandro in a dream. She begged him to let go of his anger and to change his life. By a special grace, Alessandro listened and was healed. In accepting Maria's forgiveness, he also learned to forgive; he learned to let go of the darkness he had been clinging to so tightly.

Are we not all a little like Alessandro? Our pride makes us cling to our anger. Perhaps we were wronged; perhaps our life was changed, derailed, or even destroyed by the actions of another who remains unrepentant and indifferent to our fate. Perhaps we have many reasons to cherish a secret rage or a lingering resentment. Perhaps the one we find it hardest to forgive is ourselves. And in response to the hurt we have suffered, we want to inflict it on others.

But the ones who suffer most from unforgiveness are us. Why not let go of pride and anger, and trust God to heal the wounds in your soul? He can make lilies grow where bleeding holes were. He can turn a tragedy into a path of growth. But He cannot do it unless we open the door and let His forgiveness become our forgiveness. Once we do, God alone knows what miracles He can work.

Alessandro and Maria's mother were reconciled, and he eventually became a lay brother with the Order of Friars Minor Capuchin. There he worked as a receptionist, welcoming people, and as a gardener. He even attended Maria's canonization in Rome in 1950. Twenty years later, he died of old age, in peace. Forgiveness is a powerful thing.

In what way does our choice to forgive (or not to forgive) affect "who we want to be, how we want to live, and how we want to die"?

Conclusion

When we fail to forgive, we end up weighted down by past hurt and resentment. It becomes a burden that we carry wherever we go. Energy that could have been used to love others and be a change for good is used up.

There is a desperate need around us for voices that bring reconciliation and healing. But we all have limited resources. In order to be Christ's hands and feet in places that desperately need to see something different—a love that is supernatural and reflects HIM—we have to lay down the past. It all boils down to what we choose. What do we want more? To nurse our resentment, or to be the change we want to see in the world?

When the Allied soldiers found the Nazi concentration camp at Ravensbrück, where about ninety-two thousand women and children had died, they found a note tied to a rock that had been placed next to a dead woman and child. It is actually a prayer written by one of the women:

> O Lord, when I shall come with glory into your Kingdom, remember not only the men and women of good will; remember also those of ill will. But do not only remember the suffering they have inflicted on us. Remember the fruits we bought thanks to this suffering; our comradeship, our loyalty, our humility, the courage, the generosity, the greatness of heart which have become part of our lives because of our suffering here. May the memory of us not be a nightmare to them when they stand in judgment. When they come to judgment, let all the fruits that we have borne be their forgiveness. Amen. Amen. Amen.[13]

These words render us speechless. In the face of unthinkable brutality, cruelty, and evil, a hand of mercy was extended. Those who needed this forgiveness probably never realized it had been offered. But that wasn't what mattered. The writer of these words was behind barbed wire, but in her soul, in the most valuable part of her, she was free.

---

[13] Monsignor Charles M. Mangan, "Our Grave Obligation to Forgive," *Catholic Online*, January 29, 2006, http://http://www.catholic.org/featured/headline.php?ID=2950.

My Resolution

In what specific way will I apply what I have learned in this lesson?

Examples:

1. Before I attempt to forgive another for the sins she or he has committed against me, I will examine my conscience and ask our Lord to forgive me for the sins I have committed against Him and others.

2. I will pray the Our Father, reflecting on how I would wish God to judge me, and then I will apply the same standard of mercy to those by whom I have been wronged.

3. I will read the Phases of Forgiveness (listed at the end of this section), discerning where I am in the process. I will prayerfully ask God to assist me, especially if the one I must forgive is myself.

4. If I find I cannot forgive someone no matter how hard I try, I will seek a priest, therapist, or wise spiritual counselor to assist me.

My Resolution:

Phases of Forgiveness:

1. **Uncovering:** You face the reality that you've been hurt and are angry. This is often an unfolding process. Some injuries are not absorbed all at once. It's essential to acknowledge that you have been wounded.

2. **Decision:** Will you do this your way or God's way?

3. **Work:** Just as its name implies, this phase often requires a lot of effort. This is where we put God's way into action. It may require speaking of your forgiveness to the person who wronged you, or not. It may require an effort to develop compassion for the person who has wronged you. It may require physical action.

It will require mental discipline not to put this person on trial in your mind. It will require strict obedience to God's command to forgive seventy-times-seven times. It may require going to confession. Every situation is unique. Pray, listen, and persevere.

4. **Deepening:** In this phase, we choose mercy. We ask the Lord to give us merciful hearts. We pray for the person who wronged us. Praying for our enemies is the most effective way to give God access to the parts of our hearts that are still hurting and need healing

I am not alone! God is with me every step of the way.

Catechism Clips

"And forgive us our trespasses, as we forgive those who trespass against us."

CCC 2838 This petition is astonishing. If it consisted only of the first phrase, "And forgive us our trespasses," it might have been included, implicitly, in the first three petitions of the Lord's Prayer, since Christ's sacrifice is "That sins may be forgiven." But, according to the second phrase, our petition will not be heard unless we have first met a strict requirement. Our petition looks to the future, but our response must come first, for the two parts are joined by a single word "as."

CCC 2840 Now—and this is daunting—this outpouring of mercy cannot penetrate our hearts as long as we have not forgiven those who have trespassed against us. Love, like the Body of Christ, is indivisible; we cannot love the God we cannot see if we do not love the brother or sister we do see. [See Luke 15:11–32; 18:13.] In refusing to forgive our brothers and sisters, our hearts are closed and their hardness makes them impervious to the Father's merciful love; but in confessing our sins, our hearts are opened to his grace.

CCC 2841 This petition is so important that it is the only one to which the Lord returns and which He develops explicitly in the Sermon on the Mount. [See Matthew 6:14–15; 5:23–24; Mark 11:25.] This crucial requirement of the covenant mystery is impossible for man. But "with God all things are possible." [Matthew 19:26]

CCC 2842 This "as" is not unique in Jesus' teaching: "You, therefore, must be perfect, *as* your heavenly Father is perfect"; "Be merciful, even *as* your Father is merciful"; "A new commandment I give to you, that you love one another, even *as* I have loved you, that you also love one another." [Matthew 5:48; Luke 6:36; John 13:34] It is impossible to keep the Lord's commandment by imitating the divine model from the outside; there has to be a vital participation, coming from the depths of the heart, in the holiness and the mercy and the love of our God. Only the Spirit by whom we live can make "ours" the same mind that was in Christ Jesus. [See Galatians 5:25; Philippians 2:1, 5.] Then the unity of forgiveness becomes possible and we find ourselves "forgiving one another, as God in Christ forgave" us. [Ephesians 4:32]

CCC 2843 Thus the Lord's words on forgiveness, the love that loves to the end [see John 13:1], become a living reality. The parable of the merciless servant, which crowns the Lord's teaching on ecclesial communion, ends with these words: "So also my heavenly Father will do to every one of you, if you do not forgive your brother from your heart." [See Matthew 18:23–25] It is there, in fact, "in the depths of the heart," that everything is bound and loosed. It is not in our power not to feel or to forget an offense; but the heart that offers itself to the Holy Spirit turns injury into compassion and purifies the memory in transforming the hurt into intercession.

CCC 2844 Christian prayer extends to the *forgiveness of enemies* [see Matthew 5:43–44], transfiguring the disciple by configuring him to his Master. Forgiveness is a high-point of Christian prayer; only hearts attuned to God's compassion can receive the gift of prayer. Forgiveness also bears witness that, in our world, love is stronger than sin. The martyrs of yesterday and today bear this witness to Jesus. Forgiveness is the fundamental condition of the reconciliation of the children of God with their Father and of men with one another.

CCC 2845 There is no limit or measure to this essentially divine forgiveness [see Matthew 18:21–22; Luke 17:3–4], whether one speaks of "sins" as in Luke (11:4), or "debts" as in Matthew (6:12). We are always debtors: "Owe no one anything, except to love one another." [Romans 13:8] The communion of the Holy Trinity is the source and criterion of truth in every relationship. It is lived out in prayer, above all in the Eucharist. [See Matthew 5:23–24; John 3:19–24.]

> God does not accept the sacrifice of a sower of disunion, but commands that he depart from the altar so that he may first be reconciled with his brother. For God can be appeased only by prayers that make peace. To God, the better offering is peace, brotherly accord, and a people made one in the unity of the Father, Son, and Holy Spirit.

Verse Study

See Appendix 2 for instructions on how to complete a verse study.

Matthew 6:12

1. Verse:

2. Paraphrase:

3. Questions:

4. Cross-references:

5. Personal Applications:

Write the verse on an index card and carry it with you this week.

Looking for more material? We've got you covered! Walking with Purpose meets women where they are in their spiritual journey. From our Opening Your Heart 22-lesson foundational Bible study to more advanced studies, we have something to help each and every woman grow closer to Christ. Find out more:

www.walkingwithpurpose.com

Lesson 6: Connect Coffee Talk

LOVING LIKE HIM THROUGH FORGIVENESS

Accompanying talk can be viewed by DVD or digital download purchase or access online at walkingwithpurpose.com/videos.

1. **We Have a Choice**

   A. Victim

   B. Victim plus

   "The one thing you can't take away from me is the way I choose to respond to what you do to me. The last of one's freedoms is to choose one's attitude in any given circumstance." —Viktor Frankl

2. **The Source of Forgiveness**

   We are enabled to forgive as we focus on _____.

   A. His crazy love

      Colossians 3:13: "You must make allowance for each other's faults and forgive the person who offended you. Remember the Lord forgave you, so you must forgive others."

      Matthew 6:14–15: "For if you forgive men for their transgressions, your heavenly Father will also forgive you. But if you do not forgive men, then your Father will not forgive your transgressions."

B. The forgiveness tank

It's easy to make a critical mistake about forgiveness if you start expecting the people in your life to pour back into you and refill your empty tank. Without realizing it, you begin to offer _____ forgiveness.

3. The Benefits of Forgiveness

A. Our spiritual growth

Trustful Surrender to Divine Providence:

> All that happens to us in this world against our will (whether due to men or other causes) happens to us only by the will of God, by the disposal of Providence, by His orders and under His guidance; and if from the frailty of our understanding we cannot grasp the reason for some event, let us attribute it to divine Providence, show Him respect by accepting it from His hand, believe firmly that He does not send it to us without cause.[14] —Saint Augustine

But how can a good God allow or will evil?

> In every sin, there are two parts to be distinguished, one natural and the other moral. . . . What is evil, what God couldn't cooperate with, is the sinful intention which the will of man contributes to the act. . . . As for the malice of the intention, it proceeds entirely from man and in it alone is the sinfulness in which God has no share, and yet He permits it in order to not intervene with our freedom of will.[15]

> As a surgeon who has to operate on a person of great importance takes care to cause him as little suffering as possible and only what is strictly necessary for his recovery, or as a father unwillingly punishes a son he loves dearly only because he is obliged to do so for his son's good, so God treats us as noble beings for whom he has the highest regard, or as beloved children whom he chastises because he loves them.[16]

---

[14] Father Jean Baptiste Saint-Jure and Blessed Claude de la Colombière, *Trustful Surrender to Divine Providence* (Quebec: St. Raphael Editions, 1980), 10.

[15] Ibid., 12–3.

[16] Ibid., 22–3.

All we need to think of is to keep still in His hands while He works on us, and we can rest assured that the chisel will never strike the slightest blow that is not needed for His purposes and our sanctification.[17]

B. That the world may see Christ in us

Matthew 18:23–35

Recommended Resources:

- *Lord, Heal My Hurts*, by Kay Arthur
- *From Anger to Intimacy: How Forgiveness Can Transform Your Marriage*, by Dr. Gary Smalley and Ted Cunningham
- *Trustful Surrender to Divine Providence*, by Father Jean Baptiste Saint-Jure and Blessed Claude de la Colombière

Victim Charts[18]

Victim Chart

_____

[17] Ibid., 26.
[18] Father John Hopkins, LC.

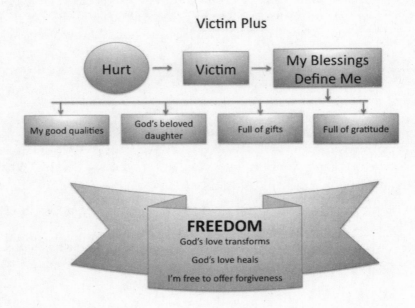

Questions for Discussion

1. True forgiveness has the following components:

    *   It is saying that you will no longer bring up the offense, play around with it in your mind, or throw it in the person's face.

    *   It is letting go of the hurt and refusing to rehearse it or rehash it in your mind.

    *   It is no longer wanting to hurt the person because he or she hurt you.

    Which of these aspects of forgiveness do you find most difficult?

2. Write down the names of three people who consistently get a rise out of you by annoying you and making you angry. Can you see any ways that God is using their presence in your life to make you more like Christ?

3. Author Kristin Armstrong writes in her book *Work in Progress*, "A woman harboring unforgiveness can appear to age a decade beyond her years." What are some other consequences of withholding forgiveness?

 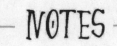 NOTES

Appendices

Appendix 1
SAINT THÉRÈSE OF LISIEUX

Patron Saint of Walking with Purpose

Saint Thérèse of Lisieux was gifted with the ability to take the riches of our Catholic faith and explain them in a way that a child could imitate. The wisdom she gleaned from Scripture ignited a love in her heart for her Lord that was personal and transforming. The simplicity of the faith that she laid out in her writings is so completely Catholic that Pope Pius XII said, "She rediscovered the Gospel itself, the very heart of the Gospel."

Walking with Purpose is intended to be a means by which women can honestly share their spiritual struggles and embark on a journey that is refreshing to the soul. It was never intended to facilitate the deepest of intellectual study of Scripture. Instead, the focus has been to help women know Christ: to know His heart, to know His tenderness, to know His mercy, and to know His love. Our logo is a little flower, and that has meaning. When a woman begins to open her heart to God, it's like the opening of a little flower. It can easily be bruised or crushed, and it must be treated with the greatest of care. Our desire is to speak to women's hearts no matter where they are in life, baggage and all, and gently introduce truths that can change their lives.

Saint Thérèse of Lisieux, the little flower, called her doctrine "the little way of spiritual childhood," and it is based on complete and unshakable confidence in God's love for us. She was not introducing new truths. She spent countless hours reading Scripture and she shared what she found, emphasizing the importance of truths that had already been divinely revealed. We can learn so much from her:

> The good God would not inspire unattainable desires; I can, then, in spite of my littleness, aspire to sanctity. For me to become greater is impossible; I must put up with myself just as I am with all my imperfections. But I wish to find the way to go to Heaven by a very straight, short, completely new little way. We are in a century of inventions: now one does not even have to take the trouble to climb the steps of a stairway; in the homes of the rich, an elevator replaces them nicely. I, too, would like to find an elevator to lift me up to Jesus, for I am too little to climb the rough stairway of perfection. So I have looked in the

books of the saints for a sign of the elevator I long for, and I have read these words proceeding from the mouth of eternal Wisdom: "He that is a little one, let him turn to me" (Proverbs 9:16). So I came, knowing that I had found what I was seeking, and wanting to know, O my God, what You would do with the little one who would answer Your call, and this is what I found:

"As one whom the mother caresses, so will I comfort you. You shall be carried at the breasts and upon the knees they shall caress you" (Isaiah 66:12–13). Never have more tender words come to make my soul rejoice. The elevator which must raise me to the heavens is Your arms, O Jesus! For that I do not need to grow; on the contrary, I must necessarily remain small, become smaller and smaller. O my God, You have surpassed what I expected, and I want to sing Your mercies. (Saint Thérèse of the Infant Jesus, *Histoire d'une Ame: Manuscrits Autobiographiques* [Paris: Éditions du Seuil, 1998], 244.)

Appendix 2
HOW TO DO A VERSE STUDY

A verse study is an exciting Bible study tool that can help to bring the Scriptures to life! By reading, reflecting on, and committing a verse to memory, we open ourselves to the Holy Spirit, who reveals very personal applications of our Lord's words and actions to our daily lives.

Learning to do a verse study is not difficult, but it can be demanding. In this Walking with Purpose™ study, a Bible verse has been selected to reinforce a theme of each lesson. To do the verse study, read the verse and then follow these simple instructions. You'll be on your way to a deeper and more personal understanding of Scripture.

- **Read the verse and the paragraph before and after the verse.**

- **Write out the selected verse.**

- **Paraphrase.**
  Write the verse using your own words. What does the verse say?

- **Ask questions.**
  Write down any questions you have about the verse. What does it say that you don't understand?

- **Use cross-references.**
  Look up other Bible verses that help to shed light on what the selected verse means. A study Bible will often list cross-references in the margin or in the study notes. Another excellent resource is Biblos.com. This website allows you to enter a specific Bible verse and it will provide many cross-references and additional insights into the passage of Scripture you selected. Record any insights you gain from the additional verses you are able to find.

- **Make a personal application.**
  What does the verse say to you personally? Is there a promise to make? a warning to heed? an example to follow? Ask God to help you find something from the verse that you can apply to your life.

The recommended Bible translations for use in Walking with Purpose™ studies are: The New American Bible, which is the translation used in the United States for the readings at Mass; The Revised Standard Version, Catholic Edition; and The Jerusalem Bible.

A SAMPLE VERSE STUDY

1. **Verse:**
John 15:5 "I am the vine, you are the branches. Those who abide in me and I in them bear much fruit, because apart from me you can do nothing."

2. **Paraphrase:**
Jesus is the vine, I am the branch. If I abide in Him, then I'll be fruitful, but if I try to do everything on my own, I'll fail at what matters most. I need Him.

3. **Questions:**
What does it mean to abide? How does Jesus abide in me? What kind of fruit is Jesus talking about?

4. **Cross-references:**
John 6:56 "He that eats my flesh, and drinks my blood, abides in me, and I in him." This verse brings to mind the Eucharist, and the importance of receiving Christ in the Eucharist as often as possible. This is a very important way to abide in Jesus.

John 15:7 "If you abide in me, and my words abide in you, ask for whatever you wish, and it will be done for you." How can Jesus' words abide in me if I never read them? I need to read the Bible if I want to abide in Christ.

John 15:16 "It was not you who chose me, but I who chose you and appointed you to go and bear fruit that will remain, so that whatever you ask the Father in my name he may give you." Not all fruit remains. Some is good only temporarily—on earth. I want my fruit to remain in eternity—to count in the long run.

Galatians 5:22–23 "The fruit of the Spirit is love, joy, peace, patience, kindness, generosity, faithfulness, gentleness, self-control." These are some of the fruits that will be seen if I abide in Christ.

5. **Personal Application:**

I will study my calendar this week, making note of where I spend my time. Is most of my time spent on things that will last for eternity (fruit that remains)? I'll reassess my priorities in light of what I find.

Appendix 3
CORRIE TEN BOOM ARTICLE

Corrie ten Boom has long been honored by evangelical Christians as an exemplar of Christian faith in action. Arrested by the Nazis along with the rest of her family for hiding Jews in their Haarlem, Netherlands, home during the Holocaust, she was imprisoned and eventually sent to the Ravensbrück concentration camp along with her beloved sister, Betsie, who perished there just days before Corrie's release on December 31, 1944. Inspired by Betsie's own example of selfless love and forgiveness amid extreme cruelty and persecution, Corrie established a postwar home for other camp survivors trying to recover from the horrors they had escaped. She went on to travel widely as a missionary, preaching God's forgiveness and the need for reconciliation. Corrie's devout moral principles were tested when, by chance, she came face-to-face in 1947 with one of her former tormentors. The following description of that experience is excerpted from her 1971 autobiography, *The Hiding Place*, written with the help of John and Elizabeth Sherrill.

I'm Still Learning to Forgive

It was in a church in Munich that I saw him, a balding heavy-set man in a gray overcoat, a brown felt hat clutched between his hands. People were filing out of the basement room where I had just spoken. It was 1947 and I had come from Holland to defeated Germany with the message that God forgives. . . .

And that's when I saw him, working his way forward against the others. One moment I saw the overcoat and the brown hat; the next, a blue uniform and a visored cap with its skull and crossbones. It came back with a rush: the huge room with its harsh overhead lights, the pathetic pile of dresses and shoes in the center of the floor, the shame of walking naked past this man. I could see my sister's frail form ahead of me, ribs sharp beneath the parchment skin. Betsie, how thin you were!

Betsie and I had been arrested for concealing Jews in our home during the Nazi occupation of Holland; the man had been a guard at Ravensbrück concentration camp where we were sent. . . .

"You mentioned Ravensbrück in your talk," he was saying. "I was a guard in there." No, he did not remember me.

"But since that time," he went on, "I have become a Christian. I know that God has forgiven me for the cruel things I did there, but I would like to hear it from your lips as well. Fraulein . . ." his hand came out . . . "will you forgive me?"

And I stood there—I whose sins had every day to be forgiven—and could not. Betsie had died in that place—could he erase her slow terrible death simply for the asking?

It could not have been many seconds that he stood there, hand held out, but to me it seemed hours as I wrestled with the most difficult thing I had ever had to do.

For I had to do it—I knew that. The message that God forgives has a prior condition: that we forgive those who have injured us. "If you do not forgive men their trespasses," Jesus says, "neither will your Father in heaven forgive your trespasses."

And still I stood there with the coldness clutching my heart. But forgiveness is not an emotion—I knew that too. Forgiveness is an act of the will, and the will can function regardless of the temperature of the heart. "Jesus, help me!" I prayed silently. "I can lift my hand, I can do that much. You supply the feeling."

And so woodenly, mechanically, I thrust my hand into the one stretched out to me. And as I did, an incredible thing took place. The current started in my shoulder, raced down my arm, sprang into our joined hands. And then this healing warmth seemed to flood my whole being, bringing tears to my eyes.

"I forgive you, brother!" I cried. "With all my heart!"

For a long moment we grasped each other's hands, the former guard and the former prisoner. I had never known God's love so intensely as I did then.[19]

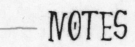 NOTES

Answer Key

NOTES

Lesson 2, Day One

1. God is *love*.
2. **A.** Patient
    B. Kind
    C. Not jealous—wants what's best for another
    D. Not boastful—focuses on others' accomplishments
    E. Not arrogant—humble
    F. Not rude—gracious
    G. Does not insist on its own way—selfless
    H. Not irritable or resentful—sweet-spirited and even-tempered
    I. Doesn't rejoice at wrong—rejoices in what's right
3. **A.** Love bears all things.
    B. Love believes all things.
    C. Love hopes all things.
    D. Love endures all things.
    E. Love never ends. Love is eternal.

Lesson 2, Day Two

1. God can no more forget us than a nursing mother can forget her child. He has written us on the palms of His hands, as proven by Christ's wounds on the cross.
2. God the Father sent Jesus into the world to save us. God's motive was totally pure. There wasn't a hidden, selfish agenda. God was motivated entirely by love for us. He longs for us, loves us, and wants to save us.
3. God continually draws us to Him because He knows that it's only through knowing and loving Him that we'll find the truth and happiness that we're all searching for. We're all created for communion with God, and our dignity is intricately tied to this. We can live a life of freedom only by acknowledging God's love and fully embracing the truth He reveals to us. God wants to give us true fulfillment in life and happiness. He knows that apart from Him, we'll settle for cheap substitutes, and never be satisfied.

Lesson 2, Day Three

1. Jesus makes it clear that He is doing the Father's will (John 10:30), speaking the Father's words (John 12:49–50), and performing the Father's miracles (John 10:32).
2. We can be ignorant of truth; we can be too attached to possessions; we can be scandalized by other believers; we can flee from God out of fear.
3. Jesus makes forgiveness, healing, and reconciliation possible. On the cross, He received the punishment for sin that we deserved, so that we could be forgiven, healed, and reconciled to our heavenly Father.

Lesson 2, Day Four

1. The father ran to his son the minute he saw him. He had no idea if his son was planning to apologize for his long absence—he ran to greet him with open arms before his son had explained his change of heart. All the father knew was that his precious son had come home. God responds to us in the same way. He isn't waiting to pounce on us

when we make mistakes. Instead, He runs to us with arms of mercy, offering us His robe of righteousness and grace.

2. The prodigal son said the right words of apology to his father, but his original motivation was sorrow over his money running out and over having to eat pig slop. The son never acknowledged how he had hurt his father, or how his own actions had affected him. The only reasons listed for his return had to do with concerns about himself: He was out of money and out of friends, suffering because of the choices he had made. He wanted to go back to his dad's estate and get what was left of what he now recognized as a really good deal, even if he had to live there as a servant. The prodigal son did not repent completely; he missed a few key elements of a thorough examination of conscience. And yet, that was still good enough for his father.

In the same way, we come back to God in various states of repentance and He never rejects us. What if I go to reconciliation to confess, "I know that what I am doing is wrong, and I don't even want to do the right thing"? This attitude is sinful—full of me—but I can go to the Father as I am. He will take the best I have to give—myself as I truly am right this minute—and bless it. He will work with me. But the misconception that we should not approach God or go to confession until we are truly and thoroughly sorry keeps us away from the Lord sometimes, when all He wants is for us to run to Him no matter what is going on in our lives. He is ready to receive us just as we are.

3. Answers will vary.

Lesson 3, Day One

1. Saint Paul considered all his worldly accolades worthless compared to the good of knowing Christ.

2. **A.** God has given each of us the ministry of reconciliation and the message of reconciliation.

   B. Answers will vary.

3. We are ambassadors for Christ, as if God were appealing through us. We are called to represent Christ to the world. If we are His ambassadors, we need to act as He would in all situations. He wants all our interactions with people to reflect His heart of mercy, kindness, and reconciliation. When we grow more and more like Jesus, allowing God to appeal to people through us, we're fulfilling our daily mission.

Lesson 3, Day Two

1. God knit you together in your mother's womb, forming your inmost being. This is the part of you—your soul—that makes you unique. God's eyes have foreseen all your actions. He formed a plan for your life before you were born.

2. No. He doesn't want us to be unaware of our spiritual gifts.

   No, there are different kinds of spiritual gifts.

   Each individual receives the manifestation of the Spirit. This means that *no child of God* is skipped over.

   The Holy Spirit is the source of the spiritual gifts; He distributes them individually as He wishes. You don't get to choose your spiritual gifts. He decides what will best equip you for the mission He calls you to in life.

3. Romans 12:6–8 lists the following spiritual gifts: prophecy, ministering, teaching, exhortation, generosity, diligent leadership, and mercy. First Corinthians 12:8–10 lists the following spiritual gifts: wisdom, knowledge, faith, healing, might deeds, prophecy, discernment of spirits, varieties of tongues, and interpretation of tongues. Ephesians 4:11 lists the following spiritual gifts: apostleship, prophecy, evangelism, teaching, and pastoring.

Lesson 3, Day Three
1. Answers will vary.
2. Answers will vary.
3. We are to take the encouragement we received from God during our difficulties, and then go to those who are hurting and offer them that same encouragement. Because we have *been there*, we are uniquely equipped to offer words of hope and comfort.
4. Answers will vary.

Lesson 3, Day Four
1. Our spiritual gifts (or charisms) have been given to us to benefit others. They are to be outwardly focused, used to build up the Church and meet the needs of the world. They should be exercised in charity; in other words, they should be used in a spirit of selfless love.
2. We begin with the attitude of a servant. We recognize that we've been given gifts for the benefits of others. We start at the bottom, serving humbly.
3. If we really want to see significant fruit come from our service, we are going to have to die to self, and that is really hard. It's a form of suffering, and we typically run from instead of toward suffering.

Lesson 4, Day One
1. According to CCC 363, the most valuable part of you is your soul, the innermost aspect of who you are. This is the part of you that is made in God's image.
2. When God looks at us, He doesn't see things the way people see them. People look at the outward appearance, but God looks at the heart.
3. The Bible teaches that a gray head is a crown of glory, not something to be ashamed of. Ideally, it's the sign of a life well lived, with growth in wisdom taking place with each passing year. Our physical bodies can be wasting away, but the inner self is renewed every day, if we will turn to God and let Him do His transforming work within us.

Lesson 4, Day Two
1. According to CCC 364, we are to "regard [our bodies] as good and to hold [them] in honor since God has created [them] and will raise [them] up on the last day.
2. Answers will vary.
3. Answers will vary.

Lesson 4, Day Three
1. My thoughts are to focus on the positive. This includes my assessments of my physical appearance.

I am to take every thought and make it captive to Christ, tearing down arguments that tempt me to consider other things more important than He.

I should not judge others, but instead should forgive them freely.

2. I am to be quick to listen, slow to speak, and slow to become angry.

I am to keep a tight rein on my tongue, or my faith won't be effective.

Whatever comes out of my mouth should build others up according to their needs. If it doesn't do that, I need to bite my tongue.

3. Answers will vary.

Lesson 4, Day Four

1. Our culture encourages us to show as much skin as looks good. By contrast, God *covers* us with a robe of salvation, wrapping us in a mantle of justice.

2. Jesus cleanses us so we can be presented with splendor, without spot or wrinkle. He offers us His righteousness so that we can be holy and without blemish. He gives us the virtue we need to be beautiful in the eyes of God.

3. Because we are part of the Church, we are the bride of Christ. Our wedding gown is made of righteous deeds. There is nothing more beautiful than a woman whose radical and sacrificial love is seen in her actions.

Lesson 5, Day One

1. When we pray the Our Father and ask for forgiveness, we're looking to a future event, because first we have to forgive the people who have hurt us. Jesus drove His point home by repeating it. He taught us to pray, "Forgive us our debts, as we have forgiven those who are in debt to us," then went back and repeated this with the words, "Yes, if you forgive others their failings, your heavenly Father will forgive you, but if you do not forgive others, your Father will not forgive your failings, either."

2. Christ's outpouring of mercy cannot penetrate our hearts as long as we have not forgiven those who have trespassed against us. When we refuse to forgive, our hearts are closed and their hardness makes them impervious to the Father's merciful love. Our hearts are opened to His grace when we confess our sins.

3. **A.** When we condemn another person, we are sitting in the seat of the Just Judge. This seat belongs to the Lord alone. Only God can see into the heart and dissect the motives of another person. Only He has the whole picture. Withholding forgiveness also implies that this person's sin makes him or her unworthy of being in the family of God. We elevate ourselves undeservedly. Are we not sinners? Christ could certainly view us in the same light, but with painful accuracy. And yet He loves to forgive us again, and again, and again. The invitation to forgive is an invitation to share in the life and nature of God.

B. When we disappoint ourselves, when we commit a sin that we thought we were too strong or faithful to do, we can become stuck in that place. It's rooted in arrogance, in a false view of our own strength. We might also be despairing that we have failed to conquer a fault that has become entrenched in our lives over time. Our self-condemnation seems justified. Perhaps we are hopeless. As humble as this may seem, it is only well-disguised pride. We are assuming that the strength, love, and mercy of God are no match for our flaws. How absurd! We must leave the timetable of progress in the Lord's hands. Holiness should not be confused with the permanent avoidance of sin, external perfection, or extraordinary feats.[20] We are successful Christians so long as we are willing to repent and receive the forgiveness of Christ each time we fall.

4. Answers will vary. When we start by seeking forgiveness from God, we are beginning with a foundation of humility. This awareness of our own propensity to make mistakes helps us to deal with others more graciously. Asking for forgiveness, even when we feel that what we did wrong is not as bad as what the other person did, often diffuses the tension. It can break down walls of defensiveness.

Lesson 5, Day Two

1. Answers will vary.
2. Answers will vary.
3. If we are going to be thinking, engaged people, then we will always be forming opinions. We can't help it. But what we do with our opinions is critical. An opinion can lead either to judgment or to intercession and loving instruction (when appropriate). When we judge, we are assuming we have all the facts, and that we can see into a person's heart. Because only God can see into the heart, we are bound to get into trouble when we do this.

Lesson 5, Day Three

1. Answers will vary.
2. **Philippians 4:8** Dwell on what is true—not what might be, what was in the past, or the worst possible scenario.
   Matthew 5:44 Pray for the person who hurt you.
   1 Corinthians 10:13 Thank God that although it is tempting to be ruled by negative thoughts and what-ifs, He can and will give us the strength to resist the temptation. Don't say, "I can't help it." With God's help, you *can* help it.
   Matthew 18:21–22 Remember that we aren't to limit the number of times we forgive. When feelings of resentment and anger take over our hearts, we can say again, "I forgive. God, help heal my hurts. I choose to forgive. Please, Lord, take care of the feelings inside me that battle with this decision."
3. The heart that offers itself to the Holy Spirit turns injury into compassion and purifies the memory in transforming the hurt into intercession.

Lesson 5, Day Four

1. Corrie ten Boom writes that her first reaction, even knowing her own need for daily forgiveness, was to say that she could not forgive. Yet she knew that she had to, that there was no choice. This wasn't a gray zone, even if what the guard had done was brutal and horrible. She writes that coldness clutched her heart, but that forgiveness is an act of the will that can function regardless of the temperature of the heart. So Corrie did her part—making the decision to forgive and lifting her hand. God did the rest. Miraculously, He poured His mercy and forgiveness into her, and she could feel the healing warmth flood her body.

---

[20] Jacques Philippe, *Interior Freedom* (New York, NY: Scepter Publishers, 2007), 42.

2. Our prayer life includes forgiving enemies. When we do this, we are changed—we become more like the Lord. The starting point is getting in tune with God's compassion. We have to first recognize that we need God's compassion and forgiveness. We aren't innocent. When we wrestle with the fact that we've been forgiven of much, we'll be better able to forgive others. When we forgive (through God's grace and help), we'll show the world that *love is stronger than sin*. What hope is found in those words! And forgiveness isn't just an add-on. It's the fundamental condition for us to reconcile with God and with one another. In God's book, forgiveness is a nonnegotiable.

3. Answers will vary.

Prayer Pages

Heavenly Father,

Draw us close to Your heart,

So we might know Your unfailing love.

You are our shelter, our refuge and safe place.

May we run to Your outstretched arms for protection.

Open our eyes to see the many ways You bless us.

Open our ears to hear Your truth and guidance.

Open our mouths to share Your mercy with others.

May we love the things that You love,

and never stray from Your side.

How high, how wide,

how deep is Your love for us!

For I am sure that neither death, nor life, nor angels, nor principalities,
nor things present, nor things to come, nor powers, nor height, nor depth,
nor anything else in all creation will be able to separate us
from the love of God in Christ Jesus our Lord.
(Romans 8:38-39)

Prayer Requests

Date:

Date:

Prayer Requests

Date:

Date:

Prayer Requests

Date:

Date:

"For to the one who has, more will be given"
Matthew 13:12

The Journey Doesn't End Here

~ Christ's Love Is Endless ~

Walking with Purpose is more than a Bible study, it's a supportive community of women seeking lasting transformation of the heart. And you are invited.

Walking with Purpose believes that change happens in the hearts of women – and, by extension, in their families and beyond – through Bible study and community. We welcome all women, irrespective of faith background, age, or marital status.

Connect with us online for regular inspiration and to join the conversation. There you'll find insightful blog posts, videos, and free scripture printables.

For a daily dose of spiritual nourishment, join our community on Facebook, Twitter, Pinterest and Instagram.

And if you're so moved to start a Walking with Purpose study group at home or in your parish, take a look at our website for more information.

walkingwithpurpose.com

walking with purpose

~ SO MUCH MORE THAN A BIBLE STUDY ~

NOTES

❋ DEEPEN YOUR FAITH ❋ OPEN YOUR ARMS ❋
❋ BROADEN YOUR CIRCLE ❋

When your heart opens, and your love for Christ deepens, you may be moved to bring Walking With Purpose to your friends or parish. It's rewarding experience for many women who, in doing so, learn to rely on God's grace while serving Him.

If leading a group seems like a leap of faith, consider that you already have all the skills you need to share the Lord's Word:

- Personal commitment to Christ
- Desire to share the love of Christ
- Belief in the power of authentic, transparent community

The Walking With Purpose community supports you with:

- Training
- Mentoring
- Bible study materials
- Promotional materials

Few things stretch and grow our faith like stepping out of our comfort zone and asking God to work through us. Say YES, soon you'll see the mysterious and unpredictable ways He works through imperfect women devoted to Him.

Remember that if you humbly offer Him what you can, He promises to do the rest.

"See to it that no one misses the grace of God" Hebrews 12:15

Learn more about bringing Walking with Purpose to your parish.
Visit us at walkingwithpurpose.com

Walking with Purpose Devotionals

Daily affirmations of God's love

Rest: 31 Days of Peace

- A beautiful, hardcover, pocket-sized devotional to take wherever you go.

- 31 Scripture-based meditations that you can read (and re-read) daily.

- Become saturated with the truth that you are seen, known, and loved by a God who gave everything for you!

Be Still: A Daily Devotional to Quiet Your Heart

- Grow closer to the Lord each day of the year with our 365-day devotional.

- This beautifully designed hardcover devotional collection will renew your mind and help you look at things from God's perspective.

- Apply what you read in *Be Still*, and you'll make significant progress in your spiritual life!

shop.walkingwithpurpose.com

walking with purpose

～ SO MUCH MORE THAN A BIBLE STUDY ～

Journal Your Prayers & Grow Closer to God

The Walking with Purpose *Praying from the Heart: Guided Journal* is a beautiful, comprehensive prayer journal that provides a private space to share your thoughts and feelings with the Lord.

Journaling your prayers lets you express a greater depth of intimacy toward God, and it will help you cultivate the practice of gratitude. Journaling will motivate you to pray regularly, too!

Praying from the Heart lays flat for easy writing, and is fashioned after the way that author Lisa Brenninkmeyer journals her own prayers. You'll love the heavyweight paper, luxurious leatherette cover, and many other special details.

shop.walkingwithpurpose.com

walking with purpose

~ SO MUCH MORE THAN A BIBLE STUDY ~

NOTES

Walking with Purpose

Seven Priorities that Make Life Work

Does your life feel out of control? Do you feel that you are doing so many things that you are doing none of them well? Did you know that Lisa Brenninkmeyer wrote a book to help you uncover the key to living a busy life with inner calm?

With humor and wisdom, Lisa will help you:

- **Stop striving and rest in God's unconditional love**
- **Experience new hope in your marriage**
- **Reach your child's heart**
- **Create clarity in a cluttered home**
- **Find friendships that go below the surface and satisfy**
- **Discover your passion and purpose**

Study Guide also Available

The book, *Walking with Purpose: Seven Priorities that Make Life Work,* and the accompanying Discussion Guide make up a 6-week study you can do on your own or with a group of friends.

Get your copy of Lisa's book,
Walking with Purpose:
Seven Priorities that Make Life Work,
at shop.walkingwithpurpose.com

walking with purpose

NOTES

blaze for Tween/Teen Girls!

*Do you want to help girls grow
in confidence, faith and kindness?*

The Lord is calling for women like you to speak truth into the hearts of young girls – girls who can be easily confused about their true worth and beauty.

BLAZE is the Walking with Purpose ministry designed especially for tween/teen girls. It makes the wisdom of the Bible relevant to the challenges girls face today, and teaches them to recognize the difference between the loving voice of their heavenly Father and the voices that tell them they aren't good enough.

You can be a positive influence on the girls you know by starting a BLAZE program for any number of girls in your parish, school or home (or use one-on-one)!

The 20-week **BLAZE Core Program** includes a Leader's Guide and fun BLAZE kits. Each kit contains a pack of Truth vs. Lie cards, materials for icebreaker activities, take-home gifts and the BLAZE Prayer Journal.

You might also like **Between You and Me**, a 40-day conversation guide for mothers and daughters to read together. The daily reflection, journaling opportunities, discussion questions, and prayer prompts will help take your relationship to a new level of honesty and intimacy.

Discovering My Purpose is a six-lesson Bible study designed to open girls' eyes to their unique purpose, gifts, and God's love. It includes the **BLAZE Spiritual Gifts Inventory**, a fabulous tool to help girls discern where God is calling them to be world-changers.

Learn more at walkingwithpurpose.com/BLAZE

"BE WHO GOD MEANT YOU TO BE
AND YOU WILL SET THE WORLD ON FIRE."
SAINT CATHERINE OF SIENA

walking with purpose

FEARLESS & FREE
EXPERIENCING HEALING AND WHOLENESS IN CHRIST

Fear is a powerful emotion, and part of the human condition. Life isn't easy. But we were never meant to go it alone. God has wired us for connection – to Him.

Do you long to be grounded in a love that will never fail you?

Fearless and Free is for any woman confronting the reality of her fears. When suffering slams into you and leaves you reeling, or you feel great one day, and down on the mat the next, turn to this Scripture study.

Do you long for healing and wholeness? Would you like to be grounded in a love that will never fail?

In these six compassionate lessons, you'll learn to:

WAKEN to the reality of who you are in Christ,

WRESTLE with the battle in your mind, and conquer the enemy who seeks to steal your true identity.

Be strengthened as a **WARRIOR** to reclaim your footing and move forward in life.

Fearless and Free is not about surviving; it's about flourishing in Christ's love, the One who truly loves you completely and without end.

Learn more about *Fearless and Free* at walkingwithpurpose.com

walking with purpose
~ SO MUCH MORE THAN A BIBLE STUDY ~

The guided tour of God's love begins here.

Opening Your Heart: The Starting Point begins a woman's exploration of her Catholic faith and enhances her relationship with Jesus Christ. This Bible study is designed to inspire thoughtful consideration of the fundamental questions of living a life in the Lord. More than anything, it's a weekly practice of opening your heart to the only One who can heal and transform lives.

Explore these topics and more:

- What is the role of the Holy Spirit in my life?
- What does the Eucharist have to do with my friendship with Christ?
- What are the limits of Christ's forgiveness?
- Why and how should I pray?
- What is the purpose of suffering?
- What challenges will I face in my efforts to follow Jesus more closely?
- How can fear be overcome?

A companion video series complements this journey with practical insights and spiritual support.

Opening Your Heart is a foundational 22-lesson Bible study that serves any woman who seeks to grow closer to God. It's an ideal starting point for women who are new to Walking with Purpose and those with prior practice in Bible study, too.

To share Walking with Purpose with the women in your parish, contact us at walkingwithpurpose.com/contact-us.

walkingwithpurpose.com

Transformative Catholic Bible Studies

Walking with Purpose Bible studies are created to help women deepen their personal relationship with Christ. Each study includes many lessons that explore core themes and challenges of modern life through the ancient wisdom of the Bible and the Catholic Church.

Opening Your Heart

A thoughtful consideration of the fundamental questions of faith – from why and how to pray to the role of the Holy Spirit in our lives and the purpose of suffering.

Living In the Father's Love

Gain a deeper understanding of how God's unconditional love transforms your relationship with others, with yourself, and most dearly, with Him.

Keeping In Balance

Discover how the wisdom of the Old and New Testaments can help you live a blessed lifestyle of calm, health, and holiness.

Touching the Divine

These thoughtful lessons draw you closer to Jesus and deepen your faith, trust, and understanding of what it means to be God's beloved daughter.

Discovering Our Dignity

Modern-day insight directly from women of the Bible presented as a tender, honest, and loving conversation—woman to woman.

Beholding His Glory

Old Testament Scripture leads us directly to our Redeemer, Jesus Christ. Page after page, God's awe-inspiring majesty is a treasure to behold.

Beholding Your King

This study of King David and several Old Testament prophets offers a fresh perspective of how all Scripture points to the glorious coming of Christ.

Grounded In Hope

Anchor yourself in the truth found in the New Testament book of Hebrews, and gain practical insight to help you run your race with perseverance.

Fearless and Free

With an emphasis on healing and wholeness, this study provides a firm foundation to stand on, no matter what life throws our way.

Reclaiming Friendship

Let God reshape how you see and experience intentional relationships, deal with your past friendship wounds, and become a woman who is capable of the lifelong bond of true friendship.

Ordering Your Priorities

An immensely practical study that will help you put the most important things first. Discover not only what matters most in life, but also how to prioritize those things!

Choose your next Bible study at shop.walkingwithpurpose.com

walking with purpose
~ SO MUCH MORE THAN A BIBLE STUDY ~

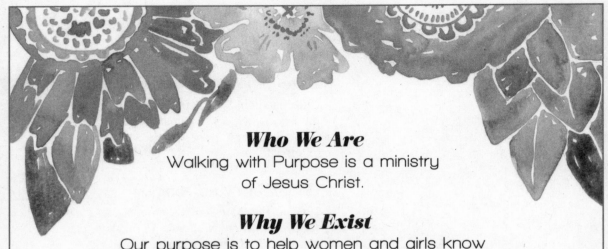

Who We Are

Walking with Purpose is a ministry
of Jesus Christ.

Why We Exist

Our purpose is to help women and girls know
Jesus Christ personally by making Scripture and the
teachings of the Catholic Church relevant and applicable.

Our Mission

Our mission is to help every Catholic woman and girl in
America encounter Jesus Christ through our Bible studies.

Our Vision

Our vision for the future is that, as more Catholic
women deepen their relationships with Jesus Christ,
eternity-changing transformation will take place in their
hearts – and, by extension – in their families, in their
communities, and ultimately, in our nation.

walking with purpose
∽ SO MUCH MORE THAN A BIBLE STUDY ∽

You can support our mission through a tax-deductible gift.
Learn more at walkingwithpurpose.com/donate